TRADEMARK
Made In America
"BLESSED" NOT CURSED!

MARY ROSS MORRIS

Copyright © 2021 by Mary Ross Morris

All rights reserved. No part of this publication may be reproduced, distributed, or transmitted in any form or by any means, including photocopying, recording, or other electronic or mechanical methods, without the prior written permission of the publisher, except in the case brief quotations embodied in critical reviews and other noncommercial uses permitted by copyright law.

ISBN: 978-1-953048-55-4 (Paperback)
        978-1-63945-220-0 (Ebook)

The views expressed in this book are solely those of the author and do not necessarily reflect the views of the publisher, and the publisher hereby disclaims any responsibility for them.

Writers' Branding
1800-608-6550
www.writersbranding.com
orders@writersbranding.com

Contents

INTRODUCTION vii

PART I

CHAPTER 1 1
  Hopes and Dreams 1
CHAPTER 2 4
  The Infamous Willie Lynch Letter 4
CHAPTER 3 15
  What Is a Curse? 15
  Universal Law of God 17
CHAPTER 4 20
  Identify Their Differences 20
  Post American Shores 20
  Fine Hair versus Coarse Hair 21
  Good Hair: The Movie 22
  Black Women and Beauty 23
  Gabrielle (Gabby) Douglas: 2012 Olympic Gold Medalist 24
  "I Love My Hair," 2010 Sesame Street 26
CHAPTER 5 29
  Light Skin versus Dark Skin 29
  Self-hatred 30
  Scenarios Shown on TV Nationwide 32
  Final and Prime Example of Self-hatred 37
  American's First President of Color: Barack Obama 40
CHAPTER 6 44
  Lies and Deception 44
  Jesus Presented to the World as White 44

    Black People, You Are Not Cursed! 50
    The Origin of Civilization 52
    Ancient Egyptians......................................54
    Invasions 55
CHAPTER 7 59
    Freedom and Equality 59
    Cases Remembered.....................................61

PART II CONTINUATION OF THE BREAKDOWN OF THE LYNCH LETTER

CHAPTER 8 67
    The Making of a Slave 67
    Frozen Psychological State of Independence 72
    Mission Accomplished 77
    A Little History on Slave Marriages: 79
CHAPTER 9 87
    The Black Female 87
    Baby Boy 87
    A New Role Reversal...................................92
    By Design 94
CHAPTER 10 99
    Conclusion: The Curse Must Be Broken 99
    Eurocentrism versus Afrocentrism 102
    Roll with It! 103
    Django Unchained 108

IN LOVING MEMORY OF 111
ACKNOWLEDGEMENT......................................112
ABOUT THE AUTHOR......................................114

This book is dedicated to all the African American mothers who have protected and shielded their sons and pushed their daughters to be successful. It is also for all those mothers who have been depleted of the love that was wholeheartedly given to the son, but the love was never given back to her in returned. This book is also dedicated to every mother who has felt the loneliness of that son's love and has battled with some type of sickness, illness, or life-threatening condition in their bodies, such as heart disease, cancer, diabetes, high blood pressure, arthritis, bursitis, and any other outward manifestation of the hurt.

It is time to awaken to the truth about this displaced relationship and to experience joy and freedom. The truth of understanding: that the love and protection you have for your son is excessive displaced emotions based on the fact that there was not a strong male figure in your life, not even the father of the son, which is also a part of the curse. It is time to reverse the curse by making the necessary changes in our lives and our psyches.

This book is dedicated to every daughter who feels less loved by their mother and who may have the potential to continue this curse with her male seed. It is time for truth and understanding of why things happened the way they did in your family relationships. Understand that you were never loved less than your male siblings; you were simply viewed as being more independent. It was never an issue of love, because love was always there.

This book is dedicated to every son who has a mother who loved him and yet, through protecting him, handicapped him into becoming a strong man while depending upon him as if he was the man in her life. Understand it was not intentionally done by the mother, but it was designed to happen, although most of us never realize the problem exists. What good is a solution if you don't know that there is a problem? To seek the change that's needed, listen with your heart.

This book is dedicated to my own daughters and sons. I love you, and I pray that this book will bring about a better understanding of why some things have turned out the way that they have. In addition, I pray that it will also bring about forgiveness for each of us. May we have the joy of understanding the truth of how this "curse" has affected each of our lives and many around us. May the truth in this book help us be free to live our best lives. Let freedom ring!

Love, Your Mother

INTRODUCTION

This book is about African Americans in America today. This book is about us. Within these pages, there will be information and facts that relate to our past and present lives, and how it has developed the experiences and culture we have today. It is my desire to provide enough information for you to get an idea of where we are headed in the future if changes are not made. This book is being written to bring about an understanding of our current identity through the historical information of our ancestors, our heritage, our culture, our lives, and our relationships. It is critical for us to understand the importance of the information in this book and how it affects our relationships with our children, parents, grandparents, siblings, and other relatives, as well as co-workers, other cultures, and nationalities that we encounter.

My initial thoughts on writing this book were to discuss the infamous Willie Lynch letter, how it brought about a curse/stigma in the lives of our ancestors (from slavery), and how it has regenerated itself into our lives today. This letter did not just appear to me, and neither did it just recently come into my possession. I had read the letter years ago and had actually kept a copy handy to show and discuss with family and friends at various times over the years. Even though it was obvious for me to see how some or all of the practices carried over into our African American culture today in some form or fashion, I didn't see how it could apply to me. There is a wise saying: "When you are ready and open to receive truth, truth will come to you." I would pray for revelations in my life. It was and still is my desire to live my life and to be an example of love and great faith while not living in deception in any area of my life. Sometimes we do things a certain way because it seems natural. We never stop to ask why we do what we do. Why do we respond or handle some things the way we do? More important, we never question why our thoughts go in a certain direction without giving them much thought?

As a single mother of four sons and two daughters, it seemed that I had more challenges with my sons than with my daughters. The challenges from the youngest to the oldest came in no particular order. My daughters were aggressive, like their mom; they observed me and followed. There was no forcing them to do anything—they simply followed through as independent young ladies. Even as children, their mothering instincts were very obvious. However, when it came to my sons, comments were made to me that I was always going out of my way to help my sons. It appeared that my sons always needed help, and it also seemed that allowances were always made for them. Therefore, this created a need for me to determine whether this reaction was conscious or unconscious, and whether those observations were really true. Did my sons need more help, and was I making allowances for them? I started to meditate in order to know truth. Then one day, the light bulb came on.

My meditations for the truth took me back to the Willie Lynch letter. The words appeared to jump off the pages when I read the part of the letter entitled "Making of a Slave." It clearly outlined what happened when they destroyed the ability of the African male slave to protect the African female slave: the outcome was "the mother will protect her sons and push her daughters to follow in her footsteps." My God! It's generations later, yet this is what was happening in my life. And through meditation, it was revealed to me that many other African American mothers were guilty of the same thing. I will speak more about this in this book, however after getting into the depths of this shocking discovery in my life, there is an overwhelming need to share this information and truth with those who have an ear to hear.

This book is being written to tell our people that we were made in America, trademarked, and stamped approved. We were part of the economic development of America by design. Our history and culture were taken from us. Our way of life became that of mimicking the slave owners and their European culture. Yes, that is a part of our history.

Many of the descendents know nothing about this part of history. Today, our young people have no interest in watching the movie *Roots* or slavery movies to learn about their history, because they simply can't relate. Yes, it is heartbreaking. Also, our young people today know nothing about segregation; they would not recognize it. They truly think they have the same opportunities and are treated equally across the board, as people of other races and nationalities. Yes, you are expected and led to think that racism is over, but in reality racism still exits and is very much alive and working in the United Stated of America and the rest of the world today.

Every day, people who are African Americans are faced with many additional challenges. And who are the challengers? Our challengers are our counterparts, who can be the whites. Blacks versus whites. How ironic that they are the number one contributor to who we are and where we are today. We have overcome many obstacles to get to where we are today. We are right beside our challengers and in front of them in some cases, desiring to be respected for how we got to our positions in life because it was a long, hard road.

We should not forget how the effects of slavery have affected whites and other non-black cultures was well. There is a "boomerang curse" effect on whites from the Lynch letter. A double-edge sword cuts both ways. This curse will also be explained and discussed later in the book, or in another book.

Here in America, we as a race of black people are involved in everything. We have recognized our first black president, although it could be more accurately stated that this is the first black president that Americans want to claim as black. Name any category, including the wealthiest of people, and African Americans are in it. But the question still lingers: Who are we?

There still appears to be an identity issue. Are we white people with darker skin? Are we the descendants of kings and queens? And what is this I hear that we strong black women don't need a man? It's also been said that black men can't deal with black women. Where did this division come from?

Many African American men and women, young and old, were interviewed to get their opinions about the various issues we face in America today. There were numerous opinions and perspectives given, and some of our people's views were simply clueless as to what is really going on. There are many issues that will be covered within the pages of this book. We have options, and we can decide who we choose to be! How do we intend to carry out a plan to reach that goal? I believe that if we can understand why we do the things we do and the fact that there is truly a root cause, then we can truly choose an option. This is our land too, because it was paid for by the lives of our ancestors and their blood, sweat, and tears. What was the reasoning behind this way of thinking to white America? To them (the powers to be), it was simple, good, economic reasoning in the building of this nation. Today, as then, black Americans cause billions of dollars to pour into America's economy. African Americans have always contributed much in this land of opportunity.

Malcolm X declared, "The common goal of 22 million African-Americans is respect as human beings, their God-given right to be a human being." Martin Luther King stated, "I have a dream that my four little children will one day live in a nation where they will not be judged by the color of our skin but by the content of their character." Can we really identify where our identity issue s are located? Why do we have this strong drive to measure up? Could it be because it is ingrained in our psyche that we don't measure up? It is my prayer that this book will open your eyes so that you may see the inner conflict each individual person faces as a member of the cultural group of black people; that freedom will truly ring in our hearts, minds, and souls; and that this identity issue will be truly settled. I believe that the right understanding can bring about changes that will continue for generations. We are truly the product of that which was manufactured in America. We have been Americanized. We are in a category all by ourselves. We know that there are those who envy us and desire to have some of the attributes that we possess, and of course, there are those who are jealous simply because they cannot keep us down. We have the opportunity to have the best America has to offer. It is up to each individual's will and determination to succeed at whatever they pursue to endeavor. We have made our own culture here in America that is specific to African Americans. We have been "Made in America" and trademarked with the American stamp of approval.

Webster's definition of trademark is "A name, symbol, or other device identifying a product, officially registered and legally restricted to the use of the owner or manufacturer, and a distinctive characteristic by which a person or thing comes to be known." Well, it is very obvious that we as African Americans have distinctive characteristics and have made our mark here in America.

Throughout this book, you will find references made to scriptures because I believe that God has given us history in the stories of the Old Testament and New Testament. Their application provides guidance and discipline for character in our lives. Every culture has their own books of stories and disciplines. I believe that the scriptures were written by inspiring men. I believe that God is still inspiring mankind today to reach His people during such a time of turmoil as these.

This book has also referenced various movies because I believe that Hollywood, the movie makers, and producers everywhere, have been very instrumental in sending a visual message to the people. Movies have the potential to stir up the viewers in a positive or negative way. This conscience of the people can set off a great unrest among the people through their emotions. I believe that a movie can be written and produced without honoring the true message that was in the mind of the writer being projected into the mind of the viewer, and what one would think is the message is really not the true message the producer had in mind. I believe this is by design. This concept is somewhat similar to subliminal messages, except the message is in the story form in the movie. I am sure that some readers will be familiar with some of the movies that are referenced; if not, hopefully they will be inspired to see them.

Television series, talk shows, and YouTube stories are also referenced in this book. These viewings and programs deal with the expressed opinions of the people and their views on a variety of subjects and issues of life. Once again, this category provides you a visual image, and it can be found on YouTube for future viewing.

In addition, within the pages of this book, I have referenced the words "white man" or "the white man." Please note that this reference *does* relates to the color of skin, because it relates to the men and women in charge of running the world, starting from the takeover of the Egyptian civilization to today. The color of their skin is considered white because these people are *not* people of color. However, they are the known wealthiest people in the world. They are the ones who truly rule the world. They call the shots about all world affairs—or should I say all affairs of the world, which of course includes those in America. (Once again, you can Google "who runs the world" and get an idea of why I used this reference.)

PART I

CHAPTER 1

Hopes and Dreams

African Americans, like all other cultures who have migrated to this country, have the same hopes and dreams of achieving the highest standard of living they can. Sometimes these desires, aspirations, hopes, and dreams are delayed, crashed, or derailed by the circumstances of life now faced here in America: the economy, which has brought many layoffs and no replacement jobs; and racism, amid the reality that even though the Emancipation Proclamation was signed, black people are still fighting for equality today. This reality is evident in today's world, where often other nationalities—even noncitizens—are hired before African Americans. The resulting unemployment creates an atmosphere inviting crime and violence in our neighborhoods. Unmet medical needs bring about a significant increase in the number of blacks with such issues as heart disease, cancer, high blood pressure, diabetes, and obesity, to name a few. These conditions cause stress to our bodies. Then there are those financially driven things in our lives that are totally out of our control. It is the proliferation of such circumstances that brings about an action and reaction in our lives and in the many lives within our culture that seem to create a unique experience within our race.

As a result, our personalities, whether they are positive or negative, are formed by these life experiences. In our need to succeed, we sometimes put undue pressure on ourselves to make things happen. What started in slavery has carried over into today's time, keeping us striving for acceptance.

When I started this book, I had to come to the conclusion that we as a people were under a curse, and my focus was centered on how to reverse the curse we live under stemming from the Willie Lynch Letter. This letter, written by William Lynch, a West Indies slave owner, was a speech said to have been delivered by him on the banks of the James River in the colony of Virginia in 1712. He had been invited to Virginia in 1712 to teach his methods of how to handle slaves. He emphatically stated that "if these principles are applied properly, it will last from 300 to 1,000 years." More than three hundred years have passed since the decree went out. It brought about a curse on our people and had an equally boomeranging effect on the white slave owners that still rears its head today.

Three hundred years is a long time, and a lot of things have changed over that period. However, some things have not changed and have simply taken on a new face, name, color, or some other characteristic prevalent today. Therefore, it is to our benefits to know the difference because our ancestors were in bondage under guidelines set forth by Willie Lynch, which created the curse that has carried over into our lives and the decisions we make today. Our actions have become the norm. Right now, you are probably wondering, "What curse? I don't have a clue about what is being discussed here." Well, don't worry, because by the end of this book, you should clearly understand the curse and how it appears today.

As previously stated, when I started this book, I was driven to identify this curse over our people and how we can break it. My research caused me to travel into the many facets of our lives as African Americans. I discovered there are already many books, YouTube videos, and articles about what is going on with our people. There are books on reversing the curse, websites with more information about the Willie Lynch letter, and speeches by well- known people and those who are trying their best to get their points across regarding the repercussions of the letter. There are also those organizations that believe that educating our people is the key to bringing about change. One organization goes from state to state and into our communities in order to teach our people about their heritage, the curse that has been passed down from generation to generation, and how to break it. The basis of this is to teach the truth so that our people can be a free people without identity issues and to help identify unresolved issues. The internet has a wealth of information. There are also books on how the psyche of the African American was affected by the Willie Lynch letter and how it is still in operation today. Many, many books are available to read and to research our background and history. This information is enlightening and will assist you in understanding why we do some of the things we do and why some thoughts are so deeply rooted in us. Some of these areas will be covered in this book; however, there is much more information available on the subject elsewhere. It is my desire to give you a hunger to know more, but more important, I want you to act on the knowledge and information given to you in this book.

I do not claim to be an expert on the subject of African Americans. However, I do understand the social dynamics that span from our beginnings here on the American continent—when our function and structure were shaped by the economic institution of slavery—to today, when these changes have left memories in our psyches that have not been erased or eliminated. I have knowledge because I am an African American woman who has lived in this society in the shadow of this three-hundred-year-old curse hovering over my life and the lives of my family and friends. I believe that now that I have identified the effect of this curse, and I am accountable to share this information. Let me share my personal experience and factual knowledge from my perspective of African Americans here in America, as well as the effects this curse has had on our lives.

CHAPTER 2

The Infamous Willie Lynch Letter

Below is a copy of the letter we are discussing. This letter has been attached in its entirety for your reading and review. It is my intention to address sections of this letter to discuss how its content is still in effect today.

The essence of this procedure and process was thorough in creating fear, distrust, and envy. It would generate division and separation that would allow slave owners control over slaves. Remember: united we stand; divided we fall. This division and separation is still relevant and in operation among our people today. This letter is specific, and I see no need to attempt to define or redefine the content. There was a game plan, and it was implemented. I believe once you read this letter with an open mind and maturity, you will start connecting the dots from over three hundred years to present day.

Willie Lynch Letter: the Making of a Slave[1]

Part 1

This speech was said to have been delivered by Willie Lynch on the bank of the James River in the colony of Virginia in 1712. Lynch was a British slave owner in the West Indies. He was invited to the

---

[1] From http://www.finalcall.com/artman/publish/Perspectives_1/Willie_Lynch_letter_The_Making_of_a_Slave.shtml

colony of Virginia in 1712 to teach his methods to slave owners there. The term "lynching" is derived from his last name.

December 25, 1712

Greetings,

Gentlemen, I greet you here on the bank of the James River in the year of our Lord one thousand seven hundred and twelve. First, I shall thank you, the gentlemen of the Colony of Virginia, for bringing me here. I am here to help you solve some of your problems with slaves. Your invitation reached me on my modest plantation in the West Indies, where I have experimented with some of the newest, and still the oldest, methods for control of slaves. Ancient Rome would envy us if my program is implemented. As our boat sailed south on the James River, named for our illustrious King, whose version of the Bible we cherish, I saw enough to know that your problem is not unique. While Rome used cords of wood as crosses for standing human bodies along its highways in great numbers, you are here using the tree and the rope on occasions. I caught the whiff of a dead slave hanging from a tree, a couple miles back. You are not only losing valuable stock by hangings, you are having uprisings, slaves are running away, your crops are sometimes left in the fields too long for maximum profit, you suffer occasional fires, your animals are killed. Gentlemen, you know what your problems are; I do not need to elaborate. I am not here to enumerate your problems, I am here to introduce you to a method of solving them. In my bag here, **I HAVE A FULL PROOF METHOD FOR CONTROLLING YOUR BLACK SLAVES**. I guarantee every one of you that, if installed correctly, **IT WILL CONTROL THE SLAVES FOR AT LEAST 300 YEARS**. My method is simple. Any member of your family or your overseer can use it. **I HAVE OUTLINED A NUMBER OF DIFFERENCES AMONG THE SLAVES; AND I TAKE THESE DIFFERENCES AND MAKE THEM BIGGER. I USE FEAR, DISTRUST AND ENVY FOR CONTROL PURPOSES.** These methods have worked on my modest plantation in the

West Indies and it will work throughout the South. Take this simple little list of differences and think about them. On top of my list is "AGE," but it's there only because it starts with an "a." The second is "COLOR" or shade. There is **INTELLIGENCE, SIZE, SEX, SIZES OF PLANTATIONS, STATUS** on plantations, **ATTITUDE** of owners, whether the slaves live in the valley, on a hill, East, West, North, South, have fine hair, course hair, or is tall or short. Now that you have a list of differences, I shall give you an outline of action, but before that, I shall assure you that **DISTRUST IS STRONGER THAN TRUST AND ENVY STRONGER THAN ADULATION, RESPECT OR ADMIRATION**. The Black slaves after receiving this indoctrination shall carry on and will become self-refueling and self-generating for **HUNDREDS** of years, maybe **THOUSANDS**. Don't forget, you must pitch the **OLD** black male vs. the **YOUNG** black male, and the **YOUNG** black male against the **OLD** black male. You must use the **DARK** skin slaves vs. the **LIGHT** skin slaves, and the **LIGHT** skin slaves vs. the **DARK** skin slaves. You must use the **FEMALE** vs. the **MALE**, and the **MALE** vs. the **FEMALE**. You must also have white servants and overseers [who] distrust all Blacks. But it is **NECESSARY THAT YOUR SLAVES TRUST AND DEPEND ON US. THEY MUST LOVE, RESPECT AND TRUST ONLY US**. Gentlemen, these kits are your keys to control. Use them. Have your wives and children use them, never miss an opportunity. **IF USED INTENSELY FOR ONE YEAR, THE SLAVES THEMSELVES WILL REMAIN PERPETUALLY DISTRUSTFUL**. Thank you gentlemen.

PART 2

LET'S MAKE A SLAVE

It was the interest and business of slave holders to study human nature, and the slave nature in particular, with a view to practical results. I and many of them attained astonishing proficiency in this direction. They had to deal not with earth, wood and stone, but with men and, by every regard, they had for their own safety and prosperity they needed to know the material on which they were to work, conscious of the injustice and wrong they were every hour perpetuating and knowing what they themselves would do. Were they the victims of such wrongs? They were constantly looking for the first signs of the dreaded retribution. They watched therefore with skilled and practiced eyes, and learned to read with great accuracy, the state of mind and heart of the slave, through his sable face. Unusual sobriety, apparent abstractions, sullenness and indifference indeed, any mood out of the common was afforded ground for suspicion and inquiry. Let us make a slave. What do we need? First of all, we need a black nigger man, a pregnant nigger woman and her baby nigger boy. Second, we will use the same basic principle that we use in breaking a horse, combined with some more sustaining factors. What we do with horses is that we break them from one form of life to another; that is, we reduce them from their natural state in nature. Whereas nature provides them with the natural capacity to take care of their offspring, we break that natural string of independence from them and thereby create a dependency status, so that we may be able to get from them useful production for our business and pleasure.

PART 3

CARDINAL PRINCIPLES FOR MAKING A NEGRO

For fear that our future generations may not understand the principles of breaking both of the beast together, the nigger and the horse. We understand that short range planning economics results in periodic economic chaos; so that to avoid turmoil in the economy, it requires us to have breadth and depth in long range comprehensive planning, articulating both skill sharp perceptions. We lay down the following principles for long range comprehensive economic planning. Both horse and niggers [are] no good to the economy in the wild or natural state. Both must be **BROKEN** and **TIED** together for orderly production. For orderly future, special and particular attention must be paid to the **FEMALE** and the **YOUNGEST** offspring. Both must be

CROSSBRED to produce a variety and division of labor. Both must be taught to respond to a peculiar new **LANGUAGE**. Psychological and physical instruction of **CONTAINMENT** must be created for both. We hold the six cardinal principles as truth to be self-evident, based upon following the discourse concerning the economics of breaking and tying the horse and the nigger together, all inclusive of the six principles laid down above. NOTE: Neither principle alone will suffice for good economics. All principles must be employed for orderly good of the nation. Accordingly, both a wild horse and a wild or natur[al] nigger is dangerous even if captured, for they will have the tendency to seek their customary freedom and, in doing so, might kill you in your sleep. You cannot rest. They sleep while you are awake, and are awake while you are asleep. They are **DANGEROUS** near the family house and it requires too much labor to watch them away from the house. Above all, you cannot get them to work in this natural state. Hence, both the horse and the nigger must be broken; that is breaking them from one form of mental life to another. **KEEP THE BODY, TAKE THE MIND!** In other words, break the will to resist. Now the breaking process is the same for both the horse and the nigger, only slightly varying in degrees. But, as we said before, there is an art in long range economic planning. **YOU MUST KEEP YOUR EYE AND THOUGHTS ON THE FEMALE and the OFFSPRING** of the horse and the nigger. A brief discourse in offspring development will shed light on the key to sound economic principles. Pay little attention to the generation of original breaking, but **CONCENTRATE ON FUTURE GENERATION**. Therefore, if you break the **FEMALE** mother, she will **BREAK** the offspring in its early years of development; and when the offspring is old enough to work, she will deliver it up to you, for her normal female protective tendencies will have been lost in the original breaking process. For example, take the case of the wild stud horse, a female horse and an already infant horse and compare the breaking process with two captured nigger males in their natural state, a pregnant nigger woman with her infant offspring. Take the stud horse, break him for limited containment. Completely break the female horse until she becomes very gentle, whereas you or anybody can ride her in her comfort. Breed the mare and the stud until you have the desired offspring. Then, you can turn the stud to freedom until you need him again. Train the female horse whereby she will eat out of your hand, and she will in turn train the infant horse to eat out of your hand, also. When it comes to breaking the uncivilized nigger, use the same process, but vary the degree and step up the pressure, so as to do a complete reversal of the mind. Take the meanest and most restless nigger, strip him of his clothes in front of the remaining male niggers, the female, and the nigger infant, tar and feather him, tie each leg to a different horse faced in opposite directions, set him afire and beat both horses to pull him apart in front of the remaining niggers. The next step is to take a bullwhip and beat the remaining nigger males to the point of death, in front of the female and the infant. Don't kill him, but **PUT THE FEAR OF GOD IN HIM**, for he can be useful for future breeding.

PART 4

THE BREAKING PROCESS OF THE AFRICAN WOMAN

Take the female and run a series of tests on her to see if she will submit to your desires willingly. Test her in every way, because she is the most important factor for good economics. If she shows any sign of resistance in submitting completely to your will, do not hesitate to use the bullwhip on her to extract that last bit of [b—] out of her. Take care not to kill her, for in doing so, you spoil good economics. When in complete submission, she will train her off springs in the early years to submit to labor when they become of age. Understanding is the best thing. Therefore, we shall go deeper into this area of the subject matter concerning what we have produced here in this breaking process of the female nigger. We have reversed the relationship; in her natural uncivilized state, she would have a strong dependency on the uncivilized nigger male, and she would have a limited protective tendency toward her independent male offspring and would raise male off springs to be dependent like her. Nature had provided for this type of balance. We reversed nature by burning and pulling a civilized nigger apart and bullwhipping the other to the point of death, all in her presence. By her being left alone, unprotected, with the **MALE IMAGE DESTROYED**, the ordeal caused her to move from her psychologically dependent state to a frozen, independent state. In this frozen, psychological state of independence, she will raise her **MALE** and female offspring in reversed roles. For **FEAR** of the young male's life, she will psychologically train him to be **MENTALLY WEAK** and **DEPENDENT**, but **PHYSICALLY STRONG**. Because she has become psychologically independent, she will train her **FEMALE** off springs to be psychologically independent. What have you got? You've got the nigger **WOMAN OUT FRONT AND THE** nigger **MAN BEHIND AND SCARED**. This is a perfect situation of sound sleep and economics. Before the breaking process, we had to be alertly on guard at all times. Now, we can sleep soundly, for out of frozen fear his woman stands guard for us. He cannot get past her early slave-molding process. He is a good tool, now ready to be tied to the horse at a tender age. By the time a nigger boy reaches the age of sixteen, he is soundly broken in and ready for a long life of sound and efficient work and the reproduction of a unit of good labor force. Continually through the breaking of uncivilized savage niggers, by throwing the nigger female savage into a frozen psychological state of independence, by killing the protective male image, and by creating a submissive dependent mind of the nigger male slave, we have created an orbiting cycle that turns on its own axis forever, unless a phenomenon occurs and re-shifts the position of the male and female slaves. We show what we mean by example. Take the case of the two economic slave units and examine them close.

PART 5

THE NEGRO MARRIAGE

We breed two nigger males with two nigger females. Then, we take the nigger male away from them and keep them moving and working. Say one nigger female bears a nigger female and the other bears a nigger male; both nigger females—being without influence of the nigger male image, frozen with a independent psychology—will raise their offspring into reverse positions. The one with the female offspring will teach her to be like herself, independent and negotiable (we negotiate with her, through her, by her, negotiates her at will). The one with the nigger male offspring, she being frozen subconscious fear for his life, will raise him to be mentally dependent and weak, but physically strong; in other words, body over mind. Now, in a few years when these two off springs become fertile for early reproduction, we will mate and breed them and continue the cycle. That is good, sound and long range comprehensive planning.

PART 6

WARNING: POSSIBLE INTERLOPING NEGATIVES

Earlier, we talked about the non-economic good of the horse and the nigger in their wild or natural state; we talked out the principle of breaking and tying them together for orderly production. Furthermore, we talked about paying particular attention to the female savage and her offspring for orderly future planning, then more recently we stated that, by reversing the positions of the male and female savages, we created an orbiting cycle that turns on its own axis forever unless a phenomenon occurred and reshifts positions of the male and female savages. Our experts warned us about the possibility of this phenomenon occurring, for they say that the mind has a strong drive to correct and re-correct itself over a period of time if it can touch some substantial original historical base; and they advised us that the best way to deal with the phenomenon is to shave off the brute's mental history and create a multiplicity of phenomena of illusions, so that each illusion will twirl in its own orbit, something similar to floating balls in a vacuum. This creation of multiplicity of phenomena of illusions entails the principle of crossbreeding the nigger and the horse as we stated above, the purpose of which is to create a diversified division of labor; thereby creating different levels of labor and different values of illusion at each connecting level of labor. The results of which is the severance of the points of original beginnings for each sphere illusion. Since we feel that the subject matter may get more complicated as we proceed in laying down our economic plan concerning the purpose, reason and effect of crossbreeding horses and niggers, we shall lay down the following definition terms for future generations. Orbiting cycle means a thing turning in a given path. Axis means upon which or around which a body turns. Phenomenon means something beyond ordinary conception and inspires awe and wonder. Multiplicity means a great number. Means a globe. Crossbreeding a horse means taking a horse and breeding it with an ass and you get a dumb, backward, ass long-headed mule that is not reproductive nor productive by itself. Crossbreeding niggers mean taking so many drops of good white blood and putting them into as many nigger women as possible, varying the drops by the various tone that you want, and then letting them breed with each other until another circle of color appears as you desire. What this means is this: Put the niggers and the horse in a breeding pot, mix some asses and some good white blood and what do you get? You got a multiplicity of colors of ass backward, unusual niggers, running, tied to backward ass long-headed mules, the one productive of itself, the other sterile. (The one constant, the other dying, we keep the nigger constant for we may replace the mules for another tool) both mule and nigger tied to each other, neither knowing where the other came from and neither productive for itself, nor without each other.

PART 7

CONTROLLED LANGUAGE

Crossbreeding completed, for further severance from their original beginning, **WE MUST COMPLETELY ANNIHILATE THE MOTHER TONGUE** of both the new nigger and the new mule, and institute a new language that involves the new life's work of both. You know language is a peculiar institution. It leads to the heart of a people. The more a foreigner knows about the language of another country the more he is able to move through all levels of that society. Therefore, if the foreigner is an enemy of the country, to the extent that he knows the body of the language, to that extent is the country vulnerable to attack or invasion of a foreign culture. For example, if you take a slave, if you teach him all about your language, he will know all your secrets, and he is then no more a slave, for you can't fool him any longer, and **BEING A FOOL IS ONE OF THE BASIC INGREDIENTS OF ANY INCIDENTS TO THE MAINTENANCE OF THE SLAVERY SYSTEM**. For example, if you told a slave that he must perform in getting out "our crops" and he knows the language well, he would know that "our crops" didn't mean "our crops" and the slavery system would break down, for he would relate on the basis of what "our crops" really meant. So you have to be careful in setting up the new language; for the slaves would soon be in your house, talking to you as "man to man" and that is death to our economic system. In addition, the definitions of words or terms are only a minute part of the process. Values are created and transported by communication through the body of the language. A total society has many interconnected value systems. All the values in the society have bridges of language to connect them for orderly working in the society. But for these language bridges, these many value systems would sharply clash and cause internal strife or civil war, the degree of the conflict being determined by the magnitude of the issues or relative opposing strength in whatever form. For example, if you put a slave in a hog pen and train him to live there and incorporate in him to value it as a way of life completely, the biggest problem you would have out of him is that he would worry you about provisions to keep the hog pen clean, or the same hog pen and make a slip and incorporate something in his language whereby he comes to value a house more than he does his hog pen, you got a problem. He will soon be in your house.

Now that you have read and reread this letter and regained your lost composure, *wow!* Yes, it is a whole lot to take in and digest at one time. I believe that reading this letter once is simply not enough to truly get a good understanding that will stick in your memory. I suggest that you digest the content of this letter in sections or in parts. Its content is deep and full of substance. My God, it was carried out, and it still working in some form today—let's just keep it real.

It has been said that this letter is a hoax. If you have any concern that it is a hoax, all I can say is check your history. All of the things outlined in this letter were applied to and implemented with the slaves. We have history with documented pictures and statements to support it. Also, William Lynch was a real person and identified as a person who owned slaves in the West Indies. In addition, if the sequence of events happened first and the letter was discovered later, it still happened and cannot be a hoax. History supports all the facts within the letter. The network media believes it, in addition to the large number of individuals and groups working to educate our people to understand their beginnings here in America and have knowledge and understanding of the who, what, when, and whys of our history.

Since this letter is so detailed, it was necessary to divide it into sections. The sections have been titled, and the letter is divided into seven parts. I'll refer to these parts in other chapters as they relate to our lives today. However, before we move into this area of reference, it is critical to have a good understanding of what a curse is and its dynamics.

CHAPTER 3

What Is a Curse?

It is crucial to understand and accept a good, clear meaning of what a curse really is. This book is written based on a curse and its effects on a group of people over a period of three hundred years, up to the year 2012. It could extend even further if it is not broken. We need to understand the following: what constituted the curse, the characteristics of a curse, and how it is implemented. It is my desire and intention to provide you with the answers to who, what, when, where, and how it came about, how it went into operation, and how to reverse and/or break this curse or defuse it in our lives. This curse caused and triggered its effects on a nation of people.

Definition of a curse: "A prayer or invocation for harm or injury to come upon one; evil or misfortune that comes as if in response to imprecation (to invoke evil on) or as retribution (the dispensing or receiving of reward or punishment in the hereafter); a cause of great harm or misfortune."

> *v.* to use profanely insolent language against, blaspheme; to call upon divine or supernatural power to send injury upon; to execrate in fervent and often profane terms; to bring great evil upon, afflict.

(Merriam-Webster.com)

The purpose of a curse: When a curse is placed on someone or something (an object), the purpose is to cause destruction, sometimes to the point of death. Because a curse is a physical action carried out by nonphysical beings (i.e., spirits), let us take a look at the definition of a spirit.

> A curse put upon a person's mind can be placed there either deliberately or unintentionally.

> Definition of a Curse (according to Biblical Terminology): Curse—to call down evil upon others violently; a call for evil to rest on someone.

Note: There are over 150 references to the word *curse* in the Bible. Without a doubt, this word existed even before the Bible. According to history, every culture has been exposed to a curse in some form or another. This word and state is not new to us. However, I will use biblical teaching and understanding relating to the state and condition of a curse and its association to the Lynch letter. You can google the word *curse* and find many definitions, explanations, and types of curses.

Because of the intent of the Willie Lynch letter, which was used to send out a decree to control slaves, the letter and its intent is against God and our God-given right to live our lives in love, peace, and harmony in the spirit of God. This decree was to control a group of people by destroying their will. The slaves were treated inhumanely. The men were compared to and treated the same as their horses in order to cause separation, strife, division, fear, distrust, envy, and much more. You read the letter. Were there any positive things mentioned? No, not one. Not only was this process successful in the making of many slaves, but in doing so, it created a group of people who became lost to who they really were in life. They were made to forget their history and who they were prior to coming to this continent, if they were to survive. Their language and culture was taken from them. I am sure by now you understand that the implementation of this process changed the psyche (or mind and spirit) of the slaves. This change of the mental state from the slaves has carried over into our lives today. How did this happen?

Universal Law of God

This universal law of God is very important to understand. There is a universal law of "Ask, and it shall be given," which means whatever we send out into the universe will return to us. Today, we use terms like "Karma is a mother" when you have sent bad or negative things out into the universe (by your speech or action), and it has come back to you. Or you might say, "You reap what you sow," which is an old saying spoken for many years. However, most people are not aware that it came from the Bible. "What goes around comes around" is another phrase based on the Bible. You have been told to watch what you say because whatever you say will come back on you.

Your spoken words are like seeds planted in the universe. And if thought on long enough, strong enough, and continuous enough, unspoken thoughts and intentions go out into the universe as planted seeds as well. Think of the universe as a garden that in time will return to you the harvest of what you sent out (or planted) into it. Words have power, and so do your thoughts.

The Bible talks about seed, time, and harvest. When a seed is planted into the ground, give it time, and it will eventually bring forth plants (i.e., harvest). Once the seed is put into the ground, there is a process that has to take place with that seed before it can come out the ground. But once the germination process is finished, it will come forth out the ground. Now, if you plant seeds for orange trees, you are not expecting to get apple trees. What will come forth is exactly what you planted; this is a universal law. Also know that the ground does not ask questions, and neither does the universe. It has its own cycle of operation, just like "What goes up must come down." This is the law of gravity. It is also a universal law. If you have any more questions about this, simply google it because there are other universal laws. It is true, and it works. Have you not heard that there is life or death in the power of the tongue? Words have creative power because we are made in the image of the creator. Therefore, we can build up or tear down with words.

When this decree went forth in words (from the Lynch letter), followed by the implementation of the process to make a slave, the seed was planted, and in time a harvest of slave-minded people was created. In addition, the curse was passed from generation to generation over hundreds of years through our people. It has been in existence so long that we as a people are not aware it even exists, simply because how we think and the way we live our lives is the norm.

Identifying the differences was the main ingredient in the process that was used to destroy the minds of the slaves by creating distrust and envy. This goes against our God-given nature.

Part One of the Lynch Letter—List of Differences

Take this simple little list of differences and think about them. On top of my list is "AGE," but it's there only because it starts with an "a." The second is "COLOR" or shade. There is **INTELLIGENCE, SIZE, SEX, SIZES OF PLANTATIONS, STATUS** on plantations, **ATTITUDE** of owners, whether the slaves live in the valley, on a hill, East, West, North, South, have fine hair, course hair, or is tall or short. Now that you have a list of differences, I shall give you an outline of action, but before that, I shall assure you that **DISTRUST IS STRONGER THAN TRUST AND ENVY STRONGER THAN ADULATION, RESPECT OR ADMIRATION**. The Black slaves after receiving this indoctrination shall carry on and will become self-refueling and self-generating for **HUNDREDS** of years, maybe **THOUSANDS**. Don't forget, you must pitch the **OLD** black male vs. the **YOUNG** black male, and the **YOUNG** black male against the **OLD** black male. You must use the **DARK** skin slaves vs. the **LIGHT** skin slaves, and the **LIGHT** skin slaves vs. the **DARK** skin slaves. You must use the **FEMALE** vs. the **MALE**, and the **MALE** vs. the **FEMALE**. You must also have white servants and overseers [who] distrust all Blacks. But it is **NECESSARY THAT YOUR SLAVES TRUST AND DEPEND ON US. THEY MUST LOVE, RESPECT AND TRUST ONLY US.** Gentlemen, these kits are your keys to control. Use them. Have your wives and children use them, never miss an opportunity. **IF USED INTENSELY FOR ONE YEAR, THE SLAVES THEMSELVES WILL REMAIN PERPETUALLY DISTRUSTFUL.** Thank you gentlemen.

This communication is coming to you on a level of your awareness. However, you will only receive what you are now ready to receive. I had to see and know the truth. It was not simply saying; "I wanted to see." I didn't want to live in deception. I had to believe it, feel it, and send out the emotions of freedom from anything that would bind me from freedom. I sent out joy and freedom. Then the answer was as clear as day—no more blurred vision.

Now, it is time to make the changes to live in the God-given joy and freedom that is my destiny. It is my desire to see other mothers, sons, and daughters have the same freedom that I am now experiencing. In addition to this generation, we not only have to concern ourselves with our children, but we have to be concerned about our grandchildren and their children. This curse has to be broken in every area of our lives.

CHAPTER 4

Identify Their Differences

The light skin versus dark skin and fine hair verses coarse hair were recorded together in the list of differences. I believe it was listed that way, because usually the lighter skinned individuals had the finest hair, and the darker skinned individual had the coarse hair. As previously stated, these issues were used as a tactic to create division, separation, and distrust. Today, because this issue is so broad and deep, we will address the issue of skin tone and texture of hair separately. Light skin versus dark skin will be more fully addressed in chapter 5. Get ready to learn more about how far back this problem began in our history and why this controversial topic is still a huge issue today.

Post American Shores

Let us go even further back, before Africans came to America and before they were enslaved. Africans had no issues with their hair and were proud of their appearances. Their hair had always been very strong and was created to withstand the conditions of their environment. Do you think for one second that they had conversations such as, "Your hair is better than mine. Your hair is longer than mine. Do you think you are better than me because your hair is longer? Do you think you are better looking because your skin is a lighter shade than mine?" Of course they did not have these thoughts or conversations, because their thinking was all about living in unity, love, and protecting their families. This type of conversations would have been unheard of.

Note: African people managed their hair by wearing many beautiful and different styles, including men who cut their hair or wore dreads. African women wore many different hairstyles, and their styles went far beyond the Afros that are worn today. For example, look up hairstyles of ancient Africa. You will be surprised that some of the same hairstyles now seen in modern America came from Africa.

Fine Hair versus Coarse Hair

Progressing Forward

In 1905, Madame C. J. Walker invented a hair softener. The first straightening comb was invented and patented by Annie Turnbo Malone in 1900. Now, think about the length of time from 1712 to 1905. That's 193 years of wearing the hairstyles that were remembered from Africa and modified in America. After almost two hundred years of slavery and forced interbreeding, there was a major change in the African American population. Many African American men, women, and children had light skin and fine hair, and they were placed in competition with those having darker skin and coarse hair. However, with the inventions of the early 1900s, African Americans are now able to soften their hair and press it out straight so that it can be worn like women who have fine hair.

Up to this time, all the black men and women were trained to know white as beautiful, followed by light-skinned blacks with white features as runner-up. This interpretation of European beauty was ingrained in them since reaching the American shores, and it was projected to all. This has been ingrained in them since reaching the American shores. Now I speak to the African Americans, now being referred to as blacks. Why not call us blacks? We are the opposite of white. In addition, out of all the nationalities in the world, we are the most like the whites because our history in American is all about mimicking them. And that's what we have done—it's undeniable.

Today, we as black women have many options for wearing our hair. We can wear wigs, weaves, extensions, hair pieces, natural styles, or whatever makes us feel good about ourselves. Feeling good about our hairstyle is important to us. When we feel that our hair is comparable to that the people from Hollywood or other famous people, we feel good. We want the same look. Today, when our hair is whipped, this makes us feel as black women that we are beautiful too. We desire to be noticed by all. The Bible says a woman's hair is her glory (beauty). We black women have taken this statement to a whole new level, where we have created a hair culture in American. It flourished because American supports free enterprise and the principle of supply and demand in an atmosphere described as the land of opportunity. Other nationalities have taken this need we have to a whole new level, and hair has become big business in America. Black Americans spend billions of dollars in the hair industry in the United States. Today, other nationalities have joined in this hair movement and are wearing wigs, weaves, and extensions. Hence that old saying, "Only my hairdresser knows for sure."

Good Hair: The Movie

Chris Rock did a documentary movie call *Good Hair*. This movie was produced to try to understand this mindset of black women regarding their hair and the great need to have hair other than their natural hair. He stated that he got the idea when his young daughter came to him and asked him, "Dad, how come I don't have good hair?"

This movie consists of a variety of interviews from black women and men, from barber shops to their clients. It touches on the first African American perm and India. It also highlights the Annual Hair Show in Atlanta, its promoters, and its participants. It is a very informative documentary. Some black women feel that this movie exposed their hair secrets. How can we be so naive to think that many are already aware of our hair secrets? The secret is well kept between the black men; it's an unspoken knowing. The attitude of the black male is to respect the fact that black women want to look good and feel good. This makes for a more pleasant relationship between the two of them. And of course, many are not aware of the things that were outlined in this movie; even many blacks will not go to see the movie. Other nationalities as well have gone to see it. From what I have seen, heard, and reviewed, the most negative comments have come from our brown-skinned sisters who are dating black men. They seem to be the most interested. After all, they are trying to follow the styles led by black women. Black women felt that this movie exposed their "secret sauce" that kept their hair looking good.

I believe it really does not matter. This movie reflects the truth about our hair history, going back to slavery and coming forward through the years to today's society. The bottom line of the movie was: (1) black women want to look good, (2) looking good means feeling good about oneself, and (3) black women will pay any price to look good. Whether that price is unaffordable or affordable, they will make a way to get the hairstyle they want. Also, this black hair market is a multi-billion-dollar market that has been created to meet the hair needs of black women specifically.

The movie ends with Christ telling his daughters, "It really doesn't matter what you do on you head; it matters what you put in your head." This thought and concept has appeared to be the missing link in the black woman's way of thinking about hair.

Black Women and Beauty

We as black women go through so much for beauty. Beauty is having our hair the way we want it, no matter the cost. We have gotten so far into the European style that we have forgotten why we didn't gave the need to hold in our culture and wear those styles that are beautiful for us with our natural hair. I can remember when we black folks would make comments about non- blacks trying to wear braids and even dreadlocks. We would say, "Oh, look at them trying to wear our hairstyles. We can't have anything without them trying to take it from us." We have forgotten we have taken and adapted to their lifestyles in every area—and in many cases, we wear it better than they do. Remember, we are the kings and queens of styles. Yet sometimes we forget that we are more like the whites than the Africans. We have been mimicking whites for hundreds of years. The practice of the cultures of slaves' native lands were denied and taken away from them, and so they were forced to forget.

Today, we blacks have not moved away from it; we simply have not embraced it. Thus, we have become more Euro-centric instead of Afro-centric. We have been in this state of thinking so long that it is burned into our psyche. This means that it is not even an afterthought in our minds. We have made comments about other minorities having an identity problem without realizing that we have failed to realize just how much of an identity problem we have. This leads me to mention the most recent hair scenario that has taken place, and I would like to bring it to black women's attention. I truly ask the question, "What were the real intentions?" I am sure with hindsight, those responses from blacks would be different.

Gabrielle (Gabby) Douglas: 2012 Olympic Gold Medalist

On August 6, 2012, a sixteen-year-old Gabby Douglas won the 2012 Olympic Gold Medal in two gymnastics categories. This was a historic win. She was the first African American to win in this category for top honors in the all-around gymnastics competition. Tears of joy welled up in my eyes. I was so happy and proud of her and of our country. So many people rejoiced around the world for her win. Yet in the middle of all this positivity, I was so disheartened to find that negative comments were being made about her hair. And no doubt, most of those comments were from our people. Why would any other nationality even care? Why was there such a need for our black women and men to overshadow her triumphs with comments about her hair? Where was the thinking?

I believe that those who commented are among the black women and men who have been overcome by the idea that hair plays such an important part in who they believe they are and their beauty. I would like to think that those who responded negatively about Gabby's hair would change their opinion once they were educated with a better understanding of the sacrifices that Gabby had to make in her life to achieve her level of success. Gabby had to put in years of daily practice for hours in order to be better than good, to be the very best in the nation.

Trademark Made In America

A statement was made about Gabby's hair being nappy and sweated out, not smooth and straight. Sweating is one of the things we all do with extensive workouts and exercise. Thank God Gabby did not allow her sweating and her hair to be a factor in her success. I would like to think that at this time, those who made the negative statements would have some heartfelt emotions and some regrets regarding their statements about her hair.

Traditionally, the natural texture and curliness of most black people's hair has not been considered beautiful in America. This setting was ripe for the negative comments about Gabby Douglas's hair. Straight, long, and bouncy hair has generally been considered fashionable, even for black people, which was confirmed by the public comments that a psychological problem exists in the minds of black people regarding their hair. There is a problem when the first major accomplishment of a national champion is not acknowledged, yet negative comments flourish. (And why wouldn't there be psychological problems for an entire race of people who were mentally and physically abused for hundreds of years, without receiving any mental health treatment or as much as a thank-you for the hardships supported by the abuse received?)

It's been more than three hundred years since the beginning of the curse of the Willie Lynch letter, yet we are so unaware of our conditioning about who we are, and we are oblivious to the fact that we are still living under this curse. So much time has passed, leaving us in this mental state. This mental state has now become the norm for most of us. Examine yourself and ask yourself: Is wearing your own natural hair an option? Can you be comfortable with wearing your own natural hair? Will you feel beautiful with your natural hair? Will wearing your hair natural reduce or increase your confidence?

Like in the case of Gabby Douglas, we criticized her hair, not that of other nationalities. We are our own worst critics. Beauty starts from within. Since I have been wearing my hair naturally, I have received lots of compliments from some blacks, but mostly from whites or other nationalities. They tell me how beautiful they think my hair is. Isn't that ironic? We are so busy trying to get our hair like theirs, and they are admiring ours. We have good, strong, healthy hair. God blessed us with it. Understand, our hair is *not* a curse. Yes, it requires work to keep it neat, but we can do it. Every nationality has to put some work into their hair. We have so many styles to choose from. But I think the main point we need to take in consideration is that we should not be in bondage by having to wear wigs, weaves, hair pieces, and extensions in order to feel good about ourselves. With this idea in mind, we should never put down our hair or speak negatively about our hair, no matter what style we wear—such as in Gabby's case. As long as the hair is clean, no matter the style, we should be able to keep things in the right perspective. Remember, we are the trendsetters.

It is a known fact that some or almost all black women have reduced their physical activities because they do not want to sweat or "mess up" their hair. Working out to reduce obesity, high blood pressure, and other physical conditions that exist among our people appears to be out of the question for some. It appears that making sure their hair looking good at all times is more important than good health. Swimming and getting in a hot tub is out of the question. We, as black women, need to reevaluate our priorities for a good, healthy life and not just focus on good hair (even if it is not our hair) that gives us a false sense of feeling good.

"I Love My Hair," 2010 Sesame Street

I would like to close out this section on fine hair and coarse hair by sharing this jingle with you from Sesame Street, entitled "I Love My Hair." It was written by Joey Mazzarino, who is white. He explained that he and his wife adopted their daughter from Ethiopia. They were unaware of how to handle her hair as she got older. He noticed that her attitude about her hair changed more when she was given a white Barbie doll. She then wanted her hair to be like the Barbie's. Seeing that this was not just an issue with his own daughter, he wrote the jingle to encourage her to like her own hair. It went viral and sent out a message to all African American women to like their own hair because it is a part of them.

The Sesame Street puppet that sang this song was a chocolate-colored female with various hair styles shown. She sings about the styles and flexibility of her hair throughout the song. Please go to YouTube to listen to the words of this jingle, along with the remix and other supporting videos. Be sure to check it out. Loving our hair is a part of loving ourselves. Why do we need someone from outside our culture to tell us that we ought to love our hair, and how versatile our hair is? This is food for thought.

I am the first to admit working with natural hair means I have to put time into it. However, with the right products, the hair is softer and more manageable. And just like training your hair to conform to the flat iron, your hair will conform to whatever styles you train it to conform to. I am wearing my hair in a loose-crinkle natural style, sometimes twisties, sometimes loose twisties, French roll, side sweep, braided up the back, down the back, and sometimes to the side. There are black beauticians who work with natural black hair only. Some beauticians have moved away from the chemicals. They try to teach our culture how this chemical damages our hair, and they offer an alternative. We all have been caught up in the chemical cycle at some point and time. But the bottom line of the chemicals is breakage and dead hair.

The key to looking beautiful is centered on how well you do your makeup. Of course, people see and feel that real beauty comes from within a person and radiates out as that person walks in love, confidence, and positivity. This means to love you first.

I am so glad that I feel free to wear my own hair. If it's necessary, I have a backup plan. As I learn more about how to work with my hair, I am so glad that my hair does not dictate my life. If I need to wear a wig, hair piece, weave, or whatever to give me the look I desire to have, I can wear this simply because that's what I chose to do. I admonish you to take the challenge and no longer be dominated by your hair. Be free. Soon you will find out and realize that nobody else really cares but you, and it is not as important as you thought it would be.

CHAPTER 5

Light Skin versus Dark Skin

The skin issue goes back more than three hundred years. There is a lot of communication regarding this issue on Google and YouTube. To my surprise, it was the comments from the younger generation discussing this issue, not the older ones. They identified that it is still an issue today. Well, that says a lot to those people who don't believe that it was passed from generation to generation. Listen, black people: this is real, and it is still as alive as it was hundreds of years ago.

It was brought out that dark-skinned black women have to work harder to compete with light-skinned black women for jobs, boyfriends, or parts in movies or videos. Today, this action by others against the dark-skinned black women is considered—and I quote—"dumb and stupid" by not just the dark- skinned black women but also the light-skinned black women. The light- skinned black woman does not want to think that a black man is only attracted to her because her skin is lighter, but there are black men who will not date black women at all. There are so many situations that are going on today in our society, and I am going to give you some stories of real-life situations for you to review and consider just how deep this issue runs in our lives today.

We as a culture of black people are loving and kindhearted already. However, for some of us, it is easier to love someone else rather than to love ourselves. Sometimes that encompasses loving the very ones who have put us down and caused us all kinds of grief. Remember, we loved their children during slavery, and even after slavery when we had the babysitting jobs and housekeeping jobs in their homes. For many years, the white images on television and magazines were the only images representing "better life" in society. These images became a model that many people imitated in real life.

I am going to use a couple of scenarios to give you an idea of how the dark skin and light skin issues are still very much an issue today. Remember, as black men and women, we have the ability to produce offspring of various shades of skin color. This has sometimes created problems within the household. As stated, the creation of light skin/fine hair and dark skin/coarse hair came into existence after the white men impregnated the African females to produce an offspring with lighter skin and finer hair. Then these light- skinned slaves mated with other light-skinned slaves, thus producing skin that was lighter, along with finer hair. This created more separation between the light-skinned and the dark-skinned slaves. They made the light-skinned slaves feel that they were special because they look more like the master and his family. The master then allowed them to come into the house to work.

Again, working in the big house also sent a message: "We are better than the other slaves." Thus, more and more division and separation was created among the slaves. In addition, this promoted an increased desire for the slaves to want to become more like the master and his wife.

Self-hatred

African American families are very familiar with the fact that they can give birth to offspring of various shades of skin color. This is common knowledge among blacks. It is a situation that is virtually not discussed because it is so common. A light-skinned black woman with a light-skinned black man can still give birth to a dark-skinned child, and vice versa. Although it is rare, it has been noted that a white women with a white man has given birth to a child with black skin color, and this is because there is black blood somewhere down the genealogical line. Maybe a great-great grandmother or grandfather had some mix during slavery times. Maybe their ancestors were black and passed for white. This is the reason for the saying that was written into law in some states: "If there is one ounce of black blood in a person, no matter how light or white that person appears to be, they are considered black." It is also a fact that a white couple that has a pure white bloodline cannot produce a child of color.

Just a side note: African Americans can also produce children with various colored eyes. I personally know a very dark-skinned black man with baby blue eyes. He said his great-great grandmother was white. My own father had light skin with freckles on his face and hazel eyes. His grandmother on his mother's side was white, and on his father's side was a Cherokee Indian. Multiply this concept with millions of Afro Americans, and it's clear that the real black culture represents a very diversified background of people.

With that idea in mind, let us combine the thoughts of the effect of self-hatred for dark skin or light skin being passed down with various shades skin to our offspring. Do you know someone who had dark skin and was treated differently when he or she was a child? I do. I think everyone probably knows people who have a story to tell about how they were treated because of the color of their skin. Do you know someone in school who was called Blackie because of very dark skin? I do. I even know someone who had several male and female children with light skin, but the youngest child's skin was dark. They called her Black. Can you imagine going through life being named Black because of the color of your skin?

Are you also aware that the opposite exists? There are light-skinned blacks who were born into a family of all darker skin parents and siblings. These siblings gave the lighter skin child a hard time. They made that child sorry he was ever born with light skin. The light-skinned child hated his skin because he was made to feel different. It certainly is a double-edged sword. I know this sounds harsh, but it is a harsh reality. Differences were made by the child's own parent. Wow! This self-hatred started back in 1712 with the programming of our ancestors that light is good and black is bad. The self-hatred continues because it is refueled by each generation as customs are passed along, and the division of black families perpetuates into the next generation via our own culture as decreed in the Lynch letter.

Remember; as black men and women, we have the ability to produce offspring of various shades of skin color, and this has created problems within the household at times. As previously stated, the creation of light skin and fine hair came into existence after the white men impregnated the African females to produce offspring with lighter skin and finer hair. Then these light-skinned slaves were mated with other light-skinned people, thus producing even lighter skinned slaves with finer hair. This created more separation between light skin and dark skin. They made the light-skinned slaves feel that they were special because they looked more like the master and his family. The master then allowed them to come into the house to work. This created more division and separation among the slaves. In addition, this also prompted slaves to want to become more like the master and his wife.

To follow is a list of various scenarios I have chosen to share with you. This should give you an idea of the magnitude reflecting just how deep this self-hatred and skin color issues remain in our society today.

Scenarios Shown on TV Nationwide

(1)   A Black Male Employee

There is a black man on the job who acts like he is white. His co-workers would say that he is an Oreo (the cookie that is black on the outside and white filling on the inside) behind his back. He plays the guitar and sings country and western music, and all of his friends are white. He has no interest in black women and has no concerns about what any black person has to say or do on the job, except his black boss. He discriminated against blacks.

One day there was a meeting with the staff that included him and other staff. At one point, a black female said something, and she touched his arm because she was standing next to him. He pulled his arm away and expressed his dissatisfaction about being touched by her. He made such a negative display of hatred and dissatisfaction about the fact that this black woman had touched him that he had to be called on the carpet by the boss. His boss explained to him that there was no place for his attitude and actions within their department and company. These actions were totally unacceptable, and if they continued, he would be terminated if they could not find another department to transfer him to. Can you even imagine that a dark-skinned black man, whose mother and siblings are black, can feel this way about black people? How can this self-hatred run so deep that it has created a self-deception as to who he really sees when he looks at himself in the mirror? This deception is so deep that it has to be spiritual.

(2) **Black Men, Check Yourself**

There are some black men who refuse to date dark-skinned black women. Why? Is it for the same reason that has already been brought out—self-hatred? In other words, he needs a lighter skinned woman to give him a feeling of superiority because she is close to being white, and that confirms acceptance for him? Well, guess what? Black women of today feel that this is "dumb and stupid." This feeling is not just felt by the dark-skinned black women but the lighter skinned women too. The light-skinned black woman does not want to think that a black man is only attracted to her because of the color of her skin. Our black women of darker skin feel that they have to work harder to compete with the lighter skinned black women for jobs, boyfriends, parts in movies, and other things. This has truly been the case for many dark-skinned black women. Look at all the light-skinned black women who have made it in all of the areas referenced above. Black men, it's time to take an evaluation test. Where is your thinking on this issue? Ask yourself if you are still stuck on beauty being light and white, or white and light is the only thing that's right. Remember that this idea and concept was planted into the psyche of your ancestors and has come forth over generations to you. Wake up! It's time to come together and stop being divided and separated because of the color of our skin. You are following the original plan that was laid out to cause division between you and the black woman. You love your mother and sisters, so love your black women. Black women in history paid a price for your freedom too.

(3) Judge Mathis

There is so much self-hatred among our culture. On *Judge Mathis*, there was a black woman who had brought her case to be heard by the judge. While expressing her case, she showed her hatred for black people. The judge questioned her and tried to get her to see that she was black and had to have so much self-hatred in order to feel the way she did. She explained that she hated their wide noses, dark skin, nappy hair, and thick lips. The judge tried to reason with her but had no such luck. She was determined that she was going to have nose surgery and lighten her skin. She refused to change her position on how she felt about blacks, but she won her case. The judge said he wasn't sure that she would accept her win because he was a black judge, and he chuckled. Everyone in the courtroom was in disbelief. Note: this self- hatred was the dialogue of her communication.

(4) *People's Court,* Judge Milian

Once again, a black woman brought her small claims court case to *People's Court* to be heard. In the process of explaining her position to the judge, she expressed she hated 90 percent of all black people. She said they were dishonest and could not be trusted. She had black male friends who were gay; she trusted them and was comfortable with them. This case was similar to the *Judge Mathis* case. This black woman expressed that she did not see herself as black. She felt she was a white woman trapped in a black woman's body. Judge Milian tried to reason with her, without any success. He tried to get her to see the self-hatred for herself that she was displaying, but she had an answer for every comment the judge made. She too won her case against her gay black friend, whom she had trusted. Once again self-hatred was the dialogue of her communication.

(5) The Montel Williams Show

A young black woman on this show expressed herself as being a white person trapped in a black body. She hated her black features. She felt that she was born in the wrong body to the wrong family. She was going to do whatever she could to be as white as she could possibly be. She did not hold anything back on her hatred for being black and for other blacks. Her total communication was as if she was a racist white. Montel had other guests speak with her to try to get her to see the self-hatred, but to no avail.

(6) Judge Alex

(3/21/2011) The same black woman that was on the Montel Williams Show, was now two years later in a courtroom show. Once again she is displayed her racist attitude towards blacks, and did not consider herself black. Judge Alex who is Cuban, tried to reason with her and some kind of sense out of the non-sense she expressed. However, the communication appeared to be going in circles. She sounded so ridiculous with her statements that she lost her case and she was asked to leave the courtroom. The black woman now appears to be an attention seeker. Who knows how she really feels? She has chosen to go on nationwide TV on more than one occasion to display her racism towards her own culture and self-hatred for herself.

(7) The Tyra Banks Show

A. On her show was a twenty-one-year-old black man who hated being black. He believed he was a white man in a black man's body of sin. He talked about his hatred for many things black, including his own features. He was very passionate about his desire to be white. He believed he could be happy if he were white, that he would have recognition if he were white.

Tyra arranged for a makeup artist to make him up as a white man with white skin and hair for one day. This young man was filmed walking down Rodeo Drive with confidence. He was friendly with white people, and they were friendly back. He even asked a white man if he could pet his dog; the white man allowed it. This young black man said he believed if he had been black, the man would not have allowed him to pet his dog, and neither would the white man have been friendly to him. At the end of the program, he stated, "This was the happiest day of my life!"

B. A young black mother had three handsome sons all under the age of seven. She was using bleaching cream on their skin to make them lighter. Her statement was, "Lighter is better." Tyra asked the mom if her kids were too young to be using bleaching cream on their skin, and if she had consulted a doctor prior to starting. First, the mother lied and said yes, she had consulted a doctor. But when Tyra challenged her on her answer, the answer changed. Tyra asked the mom if she was aware of the kind of message she was sending to her boys. She didn't respond. She was told that the message was that they are not okay or handsome unless they have lighter skin, and Tyra wondered how it would affect them when they got older. The bottom line still comes back to the mother's self-hatred for being black. The consensus is that lighter is better.

C. There was a panel of black women who wanted to be white. This was an outstanding, unbelievable show. If there was something said in the previous scenarios that were profound, wait until you hear this one. These women admitted that they had a problem, but they could not control the urges or desires to do whatever was necessary to become white or have lighter skin. Tyra had something special for them. She created a doctor's office with a surgeon, and the ladies did not know that this was a fictional setting. These ladies were interviewed individually by the so-called doctor (an actor). These women were told about the various procedures that would be necessary to bring about this lightening change. They were told horror stories about what side effects of the various applications or surgeries to make them white. Some were life- threatening, and none would leave them in good health. In addition, the procedures were very costly. At the end of the program, all of the ladies—I repeat, all of the ladies—still wanted to do the procedures. Some wanted to know how soon they could get started. They'd do whatever it took to become lighter or white. Wow, how sad. They were not even ashamed when they were told how they were willing to accept the side effects no matter how much harm it would do to their body and health. Again, this is the refueling and regenerating self-hatred.

Final and Prime Example of Self-hatred

Michael Jackson

There is no discussion or example regarding blacks and self-hatred relating to the color of their skin without including and addressing this issue as it relates to the world-famous pop star Michael Jackson. It was once said that as a child star, when he started going through puberty, his nose got larger, and he had pimples on his face. He was teased by his siblings about having a big nose, and it made him very unhappy. Thus started the beginning of his nose jobs. Then just getting a smaller nose wasn't enough, and he continued to get what we would refer to as a white person's nose. Ultimately, he finally ended up with an extremely tiny nose like a female's. He then started exploring and experimenting with lightening his skin. He worked with a dermatologist to bleach his skin to be white. Later, when he ran into problems with the bleaching, he claimed a skin disorder. When he married Lisa Presley and claimed they had sex, that was questionable. When it came to having his own children, he used the sperm of his dermatologist, who was white, and had it put into a woman who was also white, according to varying sources. This woman had children for him that were not of his sperm. Therefore, there was no black blood involved. His self-hatred was so great toward himself that he would not even use his own sperm. Again, Michael Jackson's children do not have one drop of his blood in them.

I am sure as a child star, he saw so much racism and discrimination by being in the music business, and he must have believed at an early age that white was better than black. I personally remember years ago, from watching the news when Michael was arrested on one of those occasions, that the officers made him strip down to a naked body without clothes, and they laughed and talked about the fact that his genitals were the color of a black man despite how white he looked. They were being cruel to him. I am sure that Michael Jackson experienced a lot of stress throughout his life in a black man's body despite his talent, riches, and fame. With all his fame and fortune, he was still a black man who hated himself for being black. He tried to change the external when the real issue was his state of mind about the matter.

Side Note

As you know, a lot of information can be found on Twitter, Facebook, and other websites. I read where several popular black rappers continue to make reference to "Redbone" and their preference to light-skinned women over dark-skinned woman. Once again, you need to examine your thinking on this issue. I am sure you will find that this has come from the concept that white is right and that light is better because they look closer to whites and the European look. I remembered at one time the majority of women used in music videos were light-skinned girls with long hair. I am happy to see some singers and rappers are using darker skinned women. Beauty comes in all shades of color, and when you can only see beauty as light or white, there is a problem. Also, there was a statement that certain dark-skinned rappers refuse to date or mate with a dark-skinned black woman no matter how beautiful she is, because they don't want to have dark-skinned children with nappy hair. This attitude is not any different from the scenarios previously given. Then one can understand why so many of the darker black women feel inferior to the lighter skinned black women.

Black men, you too are black. Stop downgrading your black women because of the color of their skin. They look like your mothers and sisters. Just because you are a man with dark skin and have not been hindered by the color of your skin, that does not give you the right to ignore the beauty in all shades of color. Trust me: having money does not make it right. It does not matter how wealthy you are; racism still exists. You are where you are because somewhere down the line, you are making a white man some money. So stop it. Get counseling if you see that this is a problem, and try to get this problem fixed. It is truly a big problem. The famous and well-known black people in the United States tend to set the trends for the rest of the black people and the world. Ask yourself what message you are sending.

Lines from the Martin Luther King Speech, "I Have a Dream," August 28, 1963

o I have a dream that one day this nation will rise up and live out the true meaning of its creed: "We hold these truths to be self-evident, that all men are created equal."

o I have a dream that my four little children will one day live in a nation where they will not be judged by the color of their skin but by the content of their character.

In 1963, Martin Luther King had a desire that his four little children would one day live in a nation where they would not be judged by the color of their skin but by the content of their character. That was forty-nine years ago. He was directing this speech to the white man. Yet today, the white man is not our biggest enemy. *We are our own biggest enemy.* We are doing the very thing that he was asking the white man to stop doing: stop judging ourselves by the color of our skin. Why can't we see we are still handicapping our own people because of this mindset? I hope and pray that you are able to see just how deep in our psyche this issue of the color of skin runs. Granted, we have come a long ways from slavery and the rights for independence, but we must remember that we were considered second-class citizens because of the color of our skin. There was much shedding of blood to bring about freedom for our people. We have to learn to love ourselves and teach our children and grandchildren self-love. We as a culture of black people are basically loving and kindhearted already. However, for some of us, it is easier to love someone else than to love ourselves, and sometimes that encompasses loving the very ones who have put us down and caused us all kinds of grief. Remember, we loved their children during slavery; we had no other choice, even after slavery, when we had the babysitting and housekeeping jobs in the white man's house. We are a loving and a warmhearted culture. We need to turn that love inward.

American's First President of Color: Barack Obama

American's first declared black president was elected in 2008. His father was of color, and his mother was white. He is a brown-skinned man. He is not light skin, and he cannot pass for white. His wife, Michelle, and their daughters have a chocolate skin tone. They are loved by many. In the June 4, 2013 edition of Forbes, Michelle Obama's picture was on the cover listed as; "The World's Most Powerful Black Women of 2013." They listed their annual list of the world's 100 most powerful women. There were 11 Blacks and 3 Africans and she was the first on the list.

To the ladies who desire to be white, remember that our first lady, Michelle Obama, is not using skin bleach to lighten her skin or her girls' skin. They are comfortable being themselves as the first black family in the White House. I am sure this has put a smile on the face of Martin Luther King and many others who are not here today to celebrate. President Obama's election brought tears to the eyes of millions of people, and not just blacks. This was history in the making. To top it off, in 2012 he was re-elected for another four years.

There is no greater example of freedom for black men and women than experiencing a black president of the United States. Being in bondage is a choice. Choose to love yourself. You are the only self you have. I believe that black people with a self-hatred problem about the color of their skin or their hair should ask themselves these questions:

Do you believe there is a God? Does that God make mistakes? If your answer is yes, God does make mistakes, then this means you have been deceived. Deceived by whom? The deceivers are the unseen spiritual forces carrying out the curses of division, separation, self-hatred and everything that goes with this; it has had a major effect on your psyche and how you see yourself. Think about it. Ask God or your higher self to open up the eyes of your understanding to the truth, and allow the light of truth to come in. Accept that truth and allow yourself to be free to love and be love for who you are and how you look. It's past time to be black and proud!

Side Note 1

When I was watching TV on the night of the election, there were several black women doing commentary on the events of the election and the news on various channels. I felt so proud. These women were brown or chocolate in complexion, yet they had the jobs for which they were qualified. They were not "light bright" but women of color who did an excellent job. Also, let us not forget that Los Angeles County elected the first female district attorney, and she too was a woman of color; she too made history. She was elected because of her years of experience and her tenacity to get the job done. Thank you, Dr. King, for believing and dreaming your dream. We cannot allow the efforts you made for us and your death to be in vain.

Side Note 2

Were there other black presidents? According to Google this subject of black presidents prior to Obama, is a poimt of interest. There were several undeclared black presidents. Now, this determination is based on the "one drop" rule. This was a decree that a person was black if one drop of African ancestry was in a person's lineage. This method was used during slavery and the Jim Crow period of segregation in the South, and it was supported by the Southern courts. It has been said by professional historians that if any branch of your family was here in America between the seventeenth and eighteenth centuries, it is highly likely you will find African or American Indian in the bloodline. There is much to be researched and identified regarding the presidents from the slavery period to today. Check it out; you will be surprised. In most cases, they look white, and the proof of the "one drop" was destroyed. However, there are cases where the lineage was acknowledged. Check it out for yourself.

Wake-up Call!

My prayer is that the readers of this book who know others with self-hatred about the color of their skin or the texture of their hair will share this book with them. There are no more excuses for being stuck other than the ones imposed upon the self. There is not going to be any more bloodshed for you to have freedom and love for yourself. You have imprisoned yourself. The door to your cell is closed, but it is unlocked; you can come out whenever you choose. Get yourself together mentally, walk out the door, close it behind you, and walk out the prison. You are free!

Time for Freedom: Example of the Christian Foundation

Many of my readers believe in the Bible and the stories of Jesus. Understand that the Bible is a book of discipline, and all cultures have one. However, I believe in the universal laws, which existed before any religion or Bible. Universal laws will work regardless to whether you want them to. The specific law that I am referring to is "the law of belief," which falls under the category of the universal law of attraction. Whatever you believe in, be it positive or negative, it will work for you because it will bring back to you the energy you send out of your faith, feelings, and emotions.

With that thought in mind, let me remind you that the Church teaches you through the story of the death, burial, and resurrection of Jesus, noting that his going to the cross and suffering many things delivered believers from poverty, sickness, and spiritual death. This is the foundation and belief of all Christians. Now let me ask this question: If we believe this, why are so many sick? Why are so many in poverty? According to the Bible, Jesus is not going back to Calvary because people are still sick or in poverty. There is something that must happen to each individual: it is called walking in the authority of the believer. We are to walk by faith and not by sight. We are to exercise the authority that God has given us, and we should demand whatever we need to come to us and believe it will come. Our words are like seeds, and when we speak them, they go into the soil of the universe and will bring back to us a harvest of what we sowed. It is referred to as "seed time and harvest." Plant the seed and give it time, and a harvest will come forth. We have an inheritance that was left to us. Now it is up to us to exercise our God-given right. It wasn't put into us by some religious miraculous power; we were born with the power. Now, it is time to free our minds from enslavement. Our bodies are free, but our minds are still in bondage.

CHAPTER 6

Lies and Deception

You have been brainwashed to believe that you are second-class citizens and are less intelligent, without any self-worth. Your history has been taken from you, and it has been replaced with a history of slavery and hard times. You have been told that you are not attractive with your wide nose, your big lips, your dark skin, and you kinky hair. You believed and accepted these lies. This is why it is imperative that you be educated to the truth, so that the truth can be presented to you honestly with facts. Each individual person has to seek truth. This deception has been so great in the world that there is still a certain amount of deception, even in the so-called truth and facts.

I am going to use the historical facts that have been given to us by whites and all races to prove the fallacies of the facts that have been presented to the world.

Jesus Presented to the World as White

Are you aware that "Black Jesus" is searched online nearly a million times in a month—over one thousand times per day? This tells us very clearly that others are seeking the truth.

The white man has had a need to show his control and superiority to all mankind. What greater way to do this than to show the man of all times, one of the highest profile figures in history, to be a white man called Jesus. They undermined the world by having a picture of Jesus painted with blue eyes, blond hair, and white skin. This is the image that was presented to the world. Jesus, the son of God, and all of his ancestors has been portrayed as white people. Pictures were painted and statues were erected. They were sent out to all the churches, and the world accepted the lie. This was a lie that created a great deception. The churches at that time supported the lies, and if anyone that rose against the lie, they were silenced or excommunicated. Any and all proof that this was not the case and that Jesus was indeed a black man coming from black ancestors was hidden. This deception was so great that all cultures around the world believed in the story and history of Jesus as he looked in the pictures. Even the mother of Jesus was centered on his existence as part of the white culture.

The white men of the United States destroyed it and would not photograph or paint any pictures showing black people as part of the culture of that day. This was their way of eliminating black people's place in history. This information is given during tours of the museums in Washington DC. Also, the Romans destroyed Cleopatra's statues and anything that resembled her appearance, so that she would not be remembered in history as an Egyptian (with black skin). They could present her to the world as white. Destroying the likeness seems to be a popular way the world worked in the past. Google search The Whitewashing Era and you will find once again credit being taken away from the Egyptian people.

Movie Industry

The white man was the founder of the movie industry, and so all of the biblical movies consisted of white people only—the Egyptians, Moses, Abraham, Noah, and essentially all characters from the Old and New Testaments. Why? The whites dominated the movie industry, and so they used their racist influence to portray to the world that white people were the beginning and creator of all things.

Who do you think about when you think of the following movies? *Ten Commandments, Cleopatra,* and *Pharaohs of Egypt.* Who do you think about when you think of the following biblical characters? Abraham, Noah, Joseph, Mary, Jesus, and King David. All the faces that come to your memory are white. This is certainly by design. Today, a lot of these movies have been remade. Most of them have used other nationalities than white, however they still have not given the black man and woman their place in this history. Their intentions are to show their awareness that these characters were people of color, but they still do not portray the truth.

Understand that there is absolutely no proof to support the white Jesus. The paintings, statues, movies, and whatever the white man introduced to the world is not proof. It is simply a visual lie of deception that the imprint on memory would have a longer lasting effect than any words written and read from books.

I am going to give you some factual information to educate you. Hopefully all you self-hating black people will be educated to the point that you will seek more knowledge on your own, which will build more love, respect, and self-confidence in who you really are. Blacks have often said, "We are from kings and queens." The black man has said, "I came from kings, and I am looking for my queen." This soon faded away.

I do not claim to be a black history major, but I can recognize truth when I hear and read it. Understand there is so much more. I desire to give you such an appetite and hunger to eat this truth until you are full, and you can share this food with your family, friends, and associates to bring about understanding and enlightenment of who you really are and from whom you came. We as black people have a history too. It was and still is an outstanding leadership history. We have been more advanced in many areas and the forerunner in many categories for which the white man has now taken credit. We had a history before slavery. The white man wants us to think that we had no history and that what we can claim is simply lesser intelligent Africans who lived like savages in mud huts and ran around with little to no clothes on, unlearned and ignorant. It is not true!

Biblical History

The following information is being presented to you from the information provided in biblical history. The references listed below are according to biblical scripture and not according to the account of accurate and actual history.

Examples and Biblical Proof That Jesus Was Black

Jesus was an Israelite from the tribe of Judah. The Israelites were brown- skinned (black) people.

The story of Joseph: When the sons of Israel sold their younger brother Joseph to the Egyptians, they had not seen him for many years and assumed he was dead. When famine hit their land, Israelis sent his sons to Egypt to get food. When they got to Egypt, they met their brother Joseph but did not recognize him. Joseph knew who they were, but the bottom line is that if Joseph and his brothers had been white or pale-skinned, Joseph could not have pretended to be an Egyptian (Gen. 42).

The story of Moses: Moses was born an Israelite (dark brown skin) but grew up thinking he was an Egyptian (dark brown skin). If Moses was white or of pale skin, he could have never thought he was an Egyptian (Exod. 2). Now, let us not forget that later, Moses married an Ethiopian woman. Miriam and Aaron spoke against Moses because of this marriage. This made God angry, so God caused Miriam to become leprous, white as snow. (Num. 12). The curse was turning a dark skin person white. The issue here was Moses marrying a beautiful Ethiopian woman instead of an Israelite.

The story of Jesus: When Jesus was born, because of the decree of King Herod to kill all male babies, the Lord appeared to Joseph in a dream and told him to take Mary and the child to Egypt, where they would be safe from death. If Jesus had been white, Egypt would not have been the place to hide him. Rome would have been a place more suitable to hide a white child. However, the parents would have had been white too (Matt. 2).

Christian faith advocates that Jesus was white not necessarily in words, but by promoting the white pictures and statues etc. They often diverted the attention of Jesus's skin color by saying it does not matter what color Jesus was; He came to save the world. Yet the world has been presented with a white Jesus even though the earliest images of Him clearly showed Him not to be white. When religion was brought from the black lands of Europe, Jesus and His mother were worshipped and accepted in the original form without problems. That all changed with the help of the Roman Empire, when Augustus was the leader (around 31 BC–AD 14). Most of the Eurocentric Christian world does not know the truth about the real Jesus from the tribe of Judah. Jesus was from the African continent and not from Europe. He was from the tribe of Judah (Heb. 7:14).

The Story of Samson: We all know this story. Samson was an Israelite and of Nazarite covenant. In other words, the Nazarites were the men who made commitments to God to never cut their hair or allow a razor upon their face, and there were conditions and rules that had to be followed. Samson took the Nazarite oath, yet he continually walked a thin line with those rules. You can recap the story for yourself. The point that I want to bring out is that the Bible tells us that he had seven locks of hair on his head that he had vowed not to cut. This is where his strength was, in his hair. He fell in love with the wrong woman (a Philistine harlot) who was determined to find where his strength was in order to conquer him for her people. Ultimately, he told her his secret, and she cut his seven locks. His strength left him (Judg. 16:13).

Locks: Ancient Israelites men wore locks and braids, and the Hebrew Israelites had short Afros. When the Israelites were conquered on the walls of Babylon, there were drawings showing locks on the heads of the men with wide noses, and some had musical instruments. When the two tribes of Judah were taken captive, they had painting and drawings showing their hair short and knotty, and they wore braids. The Jews and

Hebrews had Afros and the short-cropped beards of the warriors; there are pictures and paintings to support these facts. The Jamaican Israelites wear natural locks. Only woolly hair can lock. The Gentiles gave the name dreadlocks because they said they looked so dreadful. Once again, the white man is putting down the hair of the black man. Why? Because it's different from theirs and is specific to the black culture. It is a fact that if African hair is left in its natural state, it will grow long, web together and make locks. This hairstyle is still being worn in the various islands at great length. There are some men who have not cut their beards or hair, like the Nazarenes. Pictures are available online for your viewing. Our hair is special (Num. 6:5).

Here is a dictionary definition of dreadlocks: "Sometimes simply called dreads or locks are matted ropes of hair which will form on its own if the hair is allowed to grow naturally without the use of brushes, combs, razors or scissors for a long period of time. The word *locks* itself comes from the Bible."

Now, there is no way at all the straight hair of the white man can naturally make locks like that of a black man. I am sure you have seen locks on a white man before—usually a younger white man who identifies with the Rasta movement. Their locks are not started naturally; there is a component added to the hair to get it to lock. So once again, the movies have depicted Samson and Delilah as white. This cannot be true.

Referenced to Seeing Jesus:

John and Daniel described the physical features of Jesus. Reference Daniel 10:5–7, Revelation 1:14–15, and 2 Corinthians 13:1. In the mouth of two or where witnesses shall every word be established. Therefore, John and Daniel gave the same testimony.

I lifted up my eyes and looked, and behold, a man clothed in linen, whose loins were girded with pure gold of Uphaz. His body also was [a golden luster] like beryl, his face had the appearance of lightning, his eyes were like flaming torches, his arms and his feet like glowing burnished bronze, and the sound of his words was like the noise of a multitude. [Of people or the roaring of the sea]. (Dan. 10:5–7, AMP)

His head and his hairs were white like wool, as white as snow; and his eyes were as a flame of fire; and his feet like unto fine brass, as if they burned in a furnace; and his voice as the sound of many waters. (Rev. 1:14–15)

Note: Africans are the only race whose hair is like wool. In addition, the color of burned brass is dark brown. In the New Testament, Jesus is referred to in many scriptures as the Lamb of God. There are other references to Jesus as being a sheep. Could there be a coincidence that the hairs of Jesus, like our hair today, is like lamb's and sheep's hair?

At the end of the day, why do you think these errors exist? If you really think about it, you can get your head out of the sand, like I had to do in order to see and accept the truth. Truly, it's not hard to see that the origin of the man called Jesus came from two Egyptian gods, which were not white. The stories were stolen from the Egyptian library and from the hieroglyphics on the walls of the pyramids in Egypt. If you desire to know the truth, research and find it; it's waiting to be discovered. It's so easy to just go with the group; that's where one's comfort is. Religion is big business, and it is designed to keep your mind enslaved. Seek truth and you will find truth.

Black People, You Are Not Cursed!

Malcolm X, once said, "Who told you that your wide nose, big lips, and nappy hair was a curse?" Who told you that lie? Once again, the Bible misinterpreted and was used to keep the black man and woman down. And once again, we believed the lie. It was once said, "If you want to hide something from the black man, just put it in the pages of a book; he will never find it." This is referring to the fact that the white man knows that we as a race of people don't want to read. Once again, it is my intention of giving you enough information to will make you hungry enough to want more.

A friend shared with me that her cousin needed money. He claimed that he had been job hunting—unsuccessfully. My friend sent him twenty dollars inside a book on how to get prepared for job hunting. Several months passed before he found the twenty dollars. This further supports the previous statement by Malcolm X. This could also refer to the laws during slavery, which made it a crime to teach a black person reading; that law became a custom that still affects black people today, who may not give education the importance it deserves. Some don't want to be seen as smart or intelligent, which is considered white to some who are not as educated.

Curse of Leprosy

In every case of this curse, the person was made white. Leprosy is a skin condition where the person becomes white. One has to be black in order to become white. Read Leviticus 13, Numbers 12, 2 King 5, 2 Chronicles 26:16–21, and Exodus 4:6–7 for cases of leprosy.

Noah and His Three Sons

It was said that the mountain on which the Ark rested was Mt. Ararat. This is located between the Black and Caspian Seas, where the Tigris and Euphrates Rivers meet. South of this mountainous region lies the land of ancient Babylonia and Mesopotamia, where the descendants of Noah settled later.

When God restored the human race through the three sons of Noah, He clearly revealed the intention of distributing the race over the entire world. This process would later form many nationalities. Before the flood, all the people had lived in a small section of the world where the Tigris and Euphrates Rivers flowed. No one had crossed the mountains on the east or the great desert on the west.

Noah had three sons: Ham, Shem, and Japheth. The name Ham also is interpreted to say Kam, which means black. Ham had four sons, and here are their names and where they settled: Mizraim, Egypt; Cush, Ethiopia;

Canaan, Palestine; and Phut, Libya. Egypt was a part of the African branch of humanity (Gen. 10–11). Cush begat Nimrod. Nimrod became mighty on earth and instituted the Tower of Babel. Where this tower was being built and was then destroyed became known as Babylon. This is where the language was confused, and people were scattered. The reason that I shared only Ham's generation is because they all settled in places where only blacks lived at that time.

As for Noah's other sons, their wives and families moved to other parts of the country: Eastern Europe, parts of Asia, and northern Africa. In this way, the populations of the world began.

Now remember, Enoch was the great-grandfather of Noah. Seth was the son whom Adam and Eve had after Able was killed. Seth had Enoch. Enoch had a son whose name was Methuselah (the oldest man that ever lived), and he had a son named Lamech, who was the father of Noah. The reason I shared that little bit of genealogy with you is so you can see how we as black race of people go back to the original creation of man. Thus, Adam and Eve were black.

The Origin of Civilization

Scientists have long believed that modern humans were first developed in Africa and spread from there to populate the rest of the world. Richard M. Meyers of Stanford University reported this information in an issue of *Journal Science*. This conclusion was taken from a variation of 650,000 sections from DNA samples, which provided the similarities and differences between all people. To get more information on this subject, go to the Associated Press post in the February 22, 2008, edition, which gives more details to support the African origin of humans.

Scholars Have Traced the Origin of Civilization Back to a Black Woman

The skeleton frame of a black woman was found in 1988. It was determined that the age of this woman was 3.5 million years old. She was called Lucy, representing the first created woman. This skeleton was found in

Ethiopia. This fossil represented the mother of all creation. We can't very well call Lucy the mother of all creation, because now Ardi (Eve) has been found.

The oldest fossil skeleton of our human ancestor was discovered and announced by National Geographic scientists on October 1, 2009. This article goes into detail on how this fossil supersedes that of Lucy, who was up to this point considered the oldest human relative that walked the earth 3.2 million years ago. That would make this specimen 4.0–4.3 million years old. Once again, this specimen was found in Ethiopia. It was also determined that she was black. They called her Ardi. I call her Eve.

In the year 2000, the oldest remains of a child were found in Ethiopia. This child was over 3.3 million years old. It was determined that she lived 200,000 years before Lucy's lifetime. The bones are from the same species as Lucy.

Note: Ethiopians are of dark skin, and therefore Adam and Eve were black. They were mother and father, the parents of all creation. Black people should respect themselves because of it, and other nationalities should respect all people. It is important to understand that all colors of skin come from black. Black skin and dark eyes are dominant. White skin and light eyes are recessive. Thus, whites can only reproduce whiteness. In order for a white couple to have a child of color, there has to be some black blood in the DNA strain down the line somewhere. Yet a black couple can have a white baby without an interchange of white blood or DNA. There are several stories relating to these cases. In the past, Africans who gave birth to a white baby would get rid of the child or take the child away from that village, because it was seen as a curse.

Just last year, a black Nigerian couple with two existing children gave birth to a baby girl with blue eyes and blonde hair. There was no white DNA involved. Blacks have this ability. Also, there was a case in South Africa where a white couple gave birth to black daughter. It was a sad story because of racism there. She was rejected and finally ran away from home to live with other black people. She could not pass for white, yet her birth certificate and blood test proved her parents were white. Definitely there was some black blood in the DNA strains somewhere down the line. There is much that can be found on this subject. But once again, the white man does not want blacks to know the truth.

Ancient Egyptians

Ancient Egyptians existed and thrived over thousands of years before there were other races of people. This was called the golden age of Egypt. Egypt is considered the most creative, innovative, and technologically advancing civilization in human history. The Egyptians could be called the forerunner to present-day technologies. They were inventors and led in the field of science and architecture.

Accomplishments of Egyptians: The pyramids, particularly the great Pyramid of Giza, towers over monuments such as the Statue of Liberty and Big Ben. The Egyptians also created mummification, hieroglyphs, papyrus rolls, writing and language, the numerical system (1–60), the sun calendar, the plow, breath mints, bowling, having, hair cut, the door lock, toothpaste, eye makeup, clocks, ship making, navigations, birth control, automatic doors, African cosmology, astronomy, black ink, and more. They already knew about the solar system and knew that the world was round and not flat. Egyptian women created jewelry and wigs; the men boxed, fenced, and wrestled for sports. The children played board games and had dolls and had other toys. The first writing system arose out of Egypt and Mesopotamia. There are 138 known pyramids in Egypt, and pyramids in other parts of the world (this includes Mexico and South America) were erected by the Africans.

This is simply an overview; there is so much more. They already had Christianity, government, and structure, but no army. They were civilized, and there was no need for an army. They were the first, and that's why Africa is referred to as the motherland. They were the first! The ancient Egyptians civilized the world.

Trademark Made In America

Invasions

Rome invaded Egypt. The conquest of Alexander the Great brought Egypt within the orbit of the Greek world for the next nine hundred years, thereafter followed by three hundred years of rule by Macedonia. The best way I can put this is that a host of invasions took place in Africa and Egypt: Romans, Greeks, Persians, Hyksos, Muslims, Assyrians, Arabs, British, and other empires. These countries wanted the wealth of Egypt—the gold mines, the diamond mines, and everything that was of value that could be removed and returned back to their own countries as spoils. The Ancient Egyptians initially did not have an army. They were defended from attacks geography. The desert protected the flank of Egypt, northern border was protected by the Mediterranean Sea, the Nile River flowed from south to north and cataracts protected the southern borders. They were united as a people. They were ethnically and culturally unified. They were not interested in fighting; they were peace-loving people under the rule of their Pharaoh, a king who was considered a god. All of these countries and their invasions have created what you see on television as the culture of the people you see on the news fighting in the Middle East today. Every once in a while, you will see a dark-skinned person. This is not the true skin color of this country. However, because of the invasion and mix of these other cultures, in addition to the removal of so many Africans sold into slavery, you get a mixture of brown-skinned people.

Now, the white movie producers are trying to use these people and say that they were the Bible characters. Wrong again! Remember, as a nation of people, they have tried to take everything from us—*even our history*. They have made our history be their history. They have made our accomplishments be their accomplishments. It is up to us to seek the truth.

There was a huge structure made of bricks found hidden in Africa. a white man was the first to see it. However, later they tried to claim that whites had something to do with what black people had built in Africa, including the Great Pyramids of Africa (Egypt). This was the largest structure ever built south of the Nile, and it stood on behalf of a powerful black king. These kings lived in royal security, a stone-built city in the heart of Africa. The white man was so blinded by hiding his prejudice that he could not believe his eyes. Rather than face the possibility that Africans might have a history of their own, whites fabricated exotic explanations (lies and imagination). In the eighteenth and nineteenth century, Europeans chose to forget what their forebears had known very well: those kingdoms in West Africa were as lavish, splendid, and well governed as any in medieval Europe.

Blacks in Europe (Moors) were in positions of honor and distinction. Saint Maurice was a Black Martyrs (reference the history of "The Moor!") And yet the ignorant, uneducated Eurocentrics will try to tell blacks, "Black Africans only built mud huts," without realizing how utterly stupid and uneducated they look. This reminds me of King Tut's statue viewing. A white woman came to see the exhibit, and when you saw the statue, the lips and nose of the statue, she said, "Oh, my God. He was black!" Then she fainted. Some white people want to know the truth too. All people need to know the truth.

At one time, there was equality among Europeans and Africans. There were paintings of them together. What caused this change? The white man needed to lie about the great black civilization of Ancient Egypt in order to justify black slavery on planations and they never stopped lying to the world. Where ever slavery was, there was destruction. This was the destruction of the mutual respect that existed between whites and blacks. Basically, the whites' desire to increase the wealth of their countries through working slavery on various plantations was more important than the respect of black kings, queens, and knights.

Slavery/Indenture Servants of That Time

Slaves in Babylon, eighteenth century BC; slaves in Greece, seventh Century BC; slaves in Rome, second century BC; slaves in the Middle Ages, sixth through fifteenth century AD; slaves in Germany and Russia, tenth century AD; slaves in Arabia, seventh century, during the time of Muhammad.

After the collapse of the Roman Empire in the west, slavery continued in the countries around the Mediterranean. But the slaves were employed almost exclusively in households, offices, and armies. The gang slavery characteristic of large Roman estates did not reappear until the tobacco and cotton plantations of colonial America. The exception is the salt mines of the Sahara.

History is telling us that blacks have a history as rich and full of everything that would make any person of dark skin as proud as any other race. This knowledge should lift the self-image of people of color around the world as the altered history is replaced by the original and actual history.

The question is, what does this cover up have to do with the problems of race throughout the world, especially in America, the UK, South Africa, Australia, and Brazil? It's all about white control. It is critical that people of color know their history. They do not have to accept feeling like second class citizens.

The Authenticity of the Bible

In light of all the statements that I have made relating to people of color referenced in the, one must examine how these errors were made, or why they were ignored during the transcribing and portrayal of these characters. This issue has taken me back to researching the creation and origin of the Bible. Let's look at a few points.

It is known that the Bible was not written at a specific period of time; it is a compilation of many books written over a period of time by various writers. A research of the origin of the Bible and all its characters, Christianity, and the story of Jesus has been revealed through "historical facts" indicating that it was taken from stories from the library and hieroglyphics of ancient Egypt and was developed over a thousand years before it was completely released to the world. Therefore, the original characters were Egyptians (people of color), and this was hidden from the world to give credit to the Jews and white people of the world, to reduce the credit to the Ancient Egyptians, who were the first civilization on earth. The knowledge and truth that the Romans and the Greek found when they entered into Egypt was so profound that they could not allow this information to get out to the world. Thus the beginning of destroying the real and true "chosen people" of God began.

I am not here to give a history lesson on ancient Egypt, the origin of Christianity, Jesus, or any of the sort. The Internet and YouTube have plenty of information waiting for those who want to get out of the box, empty the glass of lies and deception, and fill up the glass with truth. Now, let me make it clear that I am not a Bible basher. The stories were taken from the Egyptian library from scrolls, and they gave them their characters' names. If you believe the stories, they can work for you through the universal law of belief. However, understand that you should want to know the truth and not just roll with the lie. You are God's chosen people. More and more people of all nationalities are finding out the truth, and I believe this is why we as a people have been so suppressed.

In addition, this same Bible was also used to suppress Africans here in America during slavery times and today, teaching our culture that we are like lambs when we are really like lions. It told us to obey masters while they mistreated our ancestors. It's time to wake up. You can't be set free by the truth until you figure out what lie is holding you hostage.

CHAPTER 7

Freedom and Equality

From the period slavery was abolished until today, we continue to have challenges relating to equality. Yes, we are supposed to be free, yet the total benefit that comes with this freedom has been withheld from black Americans in many areas. America morally could not continue to have slaves. The Civil War was won by those who were in favor of freedom and abolishing slavery. Yet this freedom did not come into play overnight. The fight for equality was on. Basically, the message was, "I have to lose you as a slave, but I don't have to share with you. You can never be on my level." Thus, the South created the Jim Crow laws. Segregation supposedly meant separate but equal. That was their law to justify it. They continued white superiority without labeling it that. They continued slavery by using the prison system, along with the unjust laws, to imprison black men and keep them working for free; one example is the sharecropping rules.

I can't begin to give a history lesson here; there is absolutely too much to cover. However, I would like to say that our history has consisted of hundreds of years of being made to feel like second-class citizens. We have had to fight for everything; nothing was just automatically given to us. Thank God for those men and women who have gone ahead of us to make a way for us so that we can be where we are today. There are too many names to mention and too many sequences of various civil rights movements and political events that had to take place in order for us to have the rights and privileges we have today—the rights we have in our homes, schools, churches, jobs, careers, politics, marketplace, and more. Yet there are still issues that we are continually faced with and have to deal with, and they are found under the heading of racism and discrimination.

Racism is alive and well in America. Don't think for one moment that it is just a few racists or white supremacies, because there are many. Some are in the closet, just to be safe and be politically correct. What is racism? It's when one group exhausts themselves to be superior to others. In most cases, it is the whites, which are really the minority race. They only make up one-quarter of the world's population of non-color. Three-quarters of the world's population represent people of color. Therefore the people of color are the majority. I can't tell you on a world level where the percentages of power lie, however I know at one time it was with the non-colored (i.e., whites). Yet this one-fourth has declared superiority over all other races, thus creating racism with the act of discrimination.

Now, please don't get this twisted or misunderstood. All white people are not racist, praise God! However, since slavery there are the diehards here in America. I am writing about here in American and the effect racism has had on black America. In addition, I am very much aware of racism among other cultures here in America, as well as racism in other countries. Racism has been around for thousands of years, and I believe it will never be truly eradicated. I can only hope and pray that the differences are reduced and people are drawn closer.

We as black America must not be fooled to think racism does not exist or is a little sprinkle here and there. Racism is where it has been all along in our system. It has continued to occasionally raise its head. I recently read an article that noted that there appear to be more and more cases of racism that have appeared since President Obama has been appointed president. White supremacy groups are certainly not pleased with a man of color as our nation's president, or the presence of non-white legislators. In addition, gun control (or the lack of it) remains a major problem, and there are concerns about whom the law protects.

Cases Remembered

Remember: The outcome of the Trayvon Martin case has reached worldwide attention and has brought to light how much racism is still alive here in America. He was racially profiled, which is not against the law. His acquittal had everything to do with Florida's self-defense law of "Stand Your Ground." A young man was killed, and his murder was justified. This law allows justifiable homicide. Since this law went into effect in 2005, the news reported that homicides have increased three times from previous years, and many of the victims are black.

Per a statement by Senator Chris Smith to the *Post*, "What it's done is, it has emboldened those who are sometimes looking for confrontation, because they realize they have the shield of this law. This is a classic case of, if it's my word against yours and you happen to be dead, there's no way of knowing." This lets us know that we have not arrived, that laws have to be changed. This law was also adopted by fourteen other states. I could happen in your state too.

Remember: In May 2012, a seventy-six-year-old Milwaukee white man, John Henry Spooner, fatally shot his unarmed teenage neighbor, a black boy thirteen years of age. The article that said Spooner's home had been burglarized two days before the May 2012 shooting, and he suspected thirteen-year-old Darius Simmons as a thief. He confronted the teen while the teen was taking out the trash and demanded that he return the guns. Then Spooner shot him in the chest in front of his mother when he denied stealing anything. Spooner initially thought he would plead temporary insanity, however Spooner's own home surveillance cameras captured the shooting, and prosecutors aired the footage in court. Spooner told the court he killed the boy for justice, because he believed the boy had stolen his shotguns. Look at the anger and hatred fueled by this man over his guns. There was no remorse in snuffing the life out of a black kid over a gun that could be replaced. In all probability, someone close to him took his guns. Also, Simmons's mother witnessed the shooting and was initially detained by police as her son lay dying. Once again, this reflects the system not giving consideration for the life of a young black male.

Spooner was found guilty by a jury of first-degree intentional homicide, a conviction carrying a mandatory life sentence. The option of the possibility of parole after twenty years was rejected because of Spooner's lack of remorse and desire to also kill the teen's brother. Praise God that his temporary insanity plea was shot out of the water!

Remember: Marissa Alexander was charged with three counts of aggregated assault and sentenced to twenty years in prison for firing a warning shot into the garage ceiling, in front of her abusive ex-husband. No one was hurt. Her attorney wanted a new trial based on Florida's "Stand Your Ground Law," however, the judge that was presiding over the case disagreed and would not allow the law to apply. So, the thirty-one-year-old woman was facing a mandatory twenty years in prison. Even though her husband testified under oath that he threatened to kill her and was abusive to her 9 days after she gave birth. Of course Marissa is a black woman who has never been in trouble; she has a PhD and is a great mother and stepmother. Thank God she is finally free after being behind bars for 3 years and 2 years of house detention.

Remember: In 2011 in Marietta, Georgia, a black woman, Nelson, was charged with the death of her four-year-old son, who was killed by a hit-and-run driver. The driver was given six months, and the mother was charged with second-degree vehicular homicide and other misdemeanor offenses because she didn't cross at the designated crosswalk. The bus stops were so far apart, and she would have to walk a long way from the designated stop. She crossed the street in the middle of the block. She had had a long day and had three children with her. The jury consisted of all whites, and none of them had ever ridden the bus to be able to identify with her position. There was no empathy from the jurors. Yet they did not charge the hit-and-run driver with murder. He admitted he could not see well at night, and this was not his first hit-and-run case. Yet they sentenced him to six months only.

Remember: There are several cases where black women have been sentenced to jail time for sending their children to schools outside their districts. Of course, the districts where they sent their children were predominantly white, and they wanted their children to get a better education than the school for which they were zoned. There are several scenarios for each situation. However, have you ever heard of a white woman getting arrested for sending her kids to a school out of her district, or even having the need to do it? No!

Remember: Recently a young white male singer has been noted in the news for speeding on multiple occasions. It has been said that one particular time, he was driving at high excessive speed through a gated community. At no time was he arrested. However, during this same time, a professional black athlete was stopped for speeding, and though it was not at the same excessive high speed, he was arrested.

Remember: On April 25, 2008, Sean Bell, a black twenty-three-year-old from New York City, was unarmed. He was shot fifty times on his wedding day by three NYPD detectives. One detective shot thirty-one times alone. All three detectives were acquitted of charges. The officers had opted to have a judge instead of a jury decide the case. The judge freed them.

Remember: Another case is the 1999 killing of Amador Diallo, an African immigrant who was gunned down by forty-one bullets shot by officers, who claim that they thought his wallet was a gun. This man was unarmed and innocent. He was being stopped for questioning. Once again, all officers were acquitted.

There are simply too many cases to bring to your attention regarding justice for black men and woman in America. I am sure you have some you remember. I too have many more I could discuss. It's the same old story warmed over. At the end of the day, the bottom line is to remember that racism is very much alive. It is in everything: TV, movies, sports, the corner market, the beauty supply store, the gas station, and all the places we have accepted as normal. You are still watched and followed in the stores, with redlining, profiling, and all those other titles they have for making a difference between people of color.

This racism and discrimination reminds me of the previous statement on "separate but equal" from Jim Crow. They will tell you that they are treating you equal, but they will keep you separated from them. This would be fine if we were treated equally in our separation. Now, it is obvious that the separate everything was not the same quality as white counterparts. It was second-rate everything until we said, "No more!" We will no longer accept second best, or the whites' leftovers. With separation, there is still that control over what we would get. Once the separation is removed, the playing field is leveled, and there is no need for special control because all is the same. Yet discrimination still manages to raise its ugly head. Why? Because people do not want to make changes. They want to keep us in memory that we are still inferior to them. So where are we, really? Set back two hundred years? It is the same scenario with a different twist. We will overcome this too!

Remember: We are a strong race of people. We must know who we are and be confident in who we are. The racism and discrimination that we are confronted with today is a reminder that the higher ups still want to be in control and still want to feel superior to us, no matter what the law says. Despite this attitude, we should continue to teach truth and understanding to our children. Greatness is innate in us, and we will continue to overcome the obstacles of this life. That is what this book is about.

Remember: There are many people, including whites, who are appalled by racism and discrimination. These people would like to see all of this nonsense come to an end. It takes all of us pressing together to unite against those who are in control of this system that we live in to bring about changes. We all have to be committed to a better world that can only be organized through unity.

My observation of the comments and outcry from non-blacks regarding the decision in the Trayvon Martin case left me feeling good. Some said they were ashamed to be an American; some were appalled with the justice system. These non-blacks came out and rallied for equality and justice for Trayvon Martin. They contended that there must be changes in the government, judicial system, and laws to bring about equality for all.

PART II

CONTINUATION OF THE BREAKDOWN OF THE LYNCH LETTER

CHAPTER 8

The Making of a Slave

Let us take a look at the simplest definition of a slave: "A person who is the legal property of another and is forced to obey them." Prior to this time, those being held captive to do manual labor were called many names of servitudes. However, this new word *slave* had to be established to convert a human into a piece of property.

Let's Make a Slave

It was the interest and business of slave holders to study human nature, and the slave nature in particular, with a view to practical results. I and many of them attained astonishing proficiency in this direction. They had to deal not with earth, wood and stone, but with men and, by every regard, they had for their own safety and prosperity they needed to know the material on which they were to work, conscious of the injustice and wrong they were every hour perpetuating and knowing what they themselves would do. Were they the victims of such wrongs? They were constantly looking for the first signs of the dreaded retribution. They watched therefore with skilled and practiced eyes, and learned to read with great accuracy, the state of mind and heart of the slave, through his sable face. Unusual sobriety, apparent abstractions, sullenness and indifference indeed, any mood out of the common was afforded ground for suspicion and inquiry.

> Let us make a slave. What do we need? First of all, we need a black nigger man, a pregnant nigger woman and her baby nigger boy. Second, we will use the same basic principle that we use in breaking a horse, combined with some more sustaining factors. What we do with horses is that we break them from one form of life to another; that is, we reduce them from their natural state in nature. Whereas nature provides them with the natural capacity to take care of their offspring, we break that natural string of independence from them and thereby create a dependency status, so that we may be able to get from them useful production for our business and pleasure.

This section of the Lynch letter is discussing how to make a slave, and the need to take a human being and reduce him down from his natural, God-given state to a being that is compared to that of an animal who has no spirit or soul. There was a need destroy the minds of slaves and to control them to the point that the owners could sleep at night and not live in fear. They knew that these people were people, and even though they wanted to see them as indigenous, they knew in their hearts that they were humans like them. There was this need to shear their own conscious of this idea, because prosperity and a good economy was more important to them than the people they had brought over by force and against their will. How could they possibly think that these people would be cooperative with them and their ideas, using them to develop their prosperity and economy? It was necessary to study these slaves.

No doubt the strong men tried their very best to do what they could to free themselves and their women and children. However, every attempted idea or plot was to no avail. The slaves didn't know the land or the language. I personally could not even imagine the fear and frustration these slaves went through. They tried to escape and kill their masters or whoever stood in their way. These slaves were doing exactly what anyone being held against his will would do to escape. They were simply trying to keep their sanity and identity, and not lose perception of who they really were and where they had come. They had dignity, and they were brave and bold enough to try to escape at first. This brought even more fear upon the slave owners. Therefore the slave owners had to devise a method or concept to deal with destroying the nature of the slaves. This would be for safety reasons. The slave owners had a need to destroy the will of the slaves in order to have control, which would lead to prosperity and a good economy.

For the slave owner, it was not personal; it was all about good economics. That was the primary reason the slaves were brought to America in the first place. Thus, they were to not forget. As long as they could look at the slaves as human beings who were not on their level, they reduce them down, keep them ignorant, and control them.

Cardinal Principles for Making a Negro

For fear that our future generations may not understand the principles of breaking both of the beast together, the nigger and the horse. We understand that short range planning economics results in periodic economic chaos; so that to avoid turmoil in the economy, it requires us to have breadth and depth in long range comprehensive planning, articulating both skill sharp perceptions. We lay down the following principles for long range comprehensive economic planning. Both horse and niggers [are] no good to the economy in the wild or natural state. Both must be **BROKEN** and **TIED** together for orderly production. For orderly future, special and particular attention must be paid to the **FEMALE** and the **YOUNGEST** offspring. Both must be **CROSSBRED** to produce a variety and division of labor. Both must be taught to respond to a peculiar new **LANGUAGE**. Psychological and physical instruction of **CONTAINMENT** must be created for both. We hold the six cardinal principles as truth to be self-evident, based upon following the discourse concerning the economics of breaking and tying the horse and the nigger together, all inclusive of the six principles laid down above. NOTE: Neither principle alone will suffice for good economics. All principles must be employed for orderly good of the nation. Accordingly, both a wild horse and a wild or natur[al] nigger is dangerous even if captured, for they will have the tendency to seek their customary freedom and, in doing so, might kill you in your sleep. You cannot rest. They sleep while you are awake, and are awake while you are asleep. They are **DANGEROUS** near the family house and it requires too much labor to watch them away from the house. Above all, you cannot get them to work in this natural state. Hence, both the horse and the nigger must be broken; that is breaking them from one form of mental life to another. **KEEP THE BODY, TAKE THE MIND!** In other words, break the will to resist. Now the breaking process is the same for both the horse and the nigger, only slightly varying in degrees. But, as we said before, there is an art in long range economic planning. **YOU MUST KEEP YOUR EYE AND THOUGHTS ON THE FEMALE and the OFFSPRING** of the horse and the nigger. A brief discourse in offspring development will shed light on the key to sound economic principles. Pay little attention to the generation of original breaking, but **CONCENTRATE ON FUTURE GENERATION**. Therefore, if you break the **FEMALE** mother, she will **BREAK** the offspring in its early years of development; and when the offspring is old enough to work, she will deliver it up to you, for her normal female protective tendencies will have been lost in the original breaking process. For example, take the case of the wild stud horse, a female horse and an already infant horse and compare the breaking process with two captured nigger males in their natural state, a pregnant nigger woman with her infant offspring. Take the stud horse, break him for limited containment. Completely break the female horse until she becomes very gentle, whereas you or anybody can ride her in her comfort. Breed the mare and the stud until you have the desired offspring. Then, you can turn the stud to freedom until you need him again. Train the female horse whereby she will eat out of your hand, and she will in turn train the infant horse to eat out of your hand, also. When it comes to breaking the uncivilized nigger, use the same process, but vary the degree and step up the pressure, so as to do a complete reversal of the mind. Take the meanest and most restless nigger, strip him of his clothes in front of the remaining male niggers, the female, and the nigger infant, tar and feather him, tie each leg to a different horse faced in opposite directions, set him afire and beat both horses to pull him apart in front of the remaining niggers. The next step is to take a bullwhip and beat the remaining nigger males to the point of death, in front of the female and the infant. Don't kill him, but **PUT THE FEAR OF GOD IN HIM**, for he can be useful for future breeding.

In this section, they are talking about a human, the nature of this human, and the necessity to study move of these slaves. They seek to learn their character and moods so as to prohibit any would-be negative emotions as quickly as possible. The outcome of this study was concluded because the breaking process of the slaves would be the same as that of a wild horse. This was necessary for their safety, useful production, business, and pleasure!

I will discuss what I believe are the key points focused on the "Breaking of the African Woman."

The Breaking Process of the African Woman

Take the female and run a series of tests on her to see if she will submit to your desires willingly. Test her in every way, because she is the most important factor for good economics. If she shows any sign of resistance in submitting completely to your will, do not hesitate to use the bullwhip on her to extract that last bit of [b—] out of her. Take care not to kill her, for in doing so, you spoil good economics. When in complete submission, she will train her off springs in the early years to submit to labor when they become of age. Understanding is the best thing. Therefore, we shall go deeper into this area of the subject matter concerning what we have produced here in this breaking process of the female nigger. We have reversed the relationship; in her natural uncivilized state, she would have a strong dependency on the uncivilized nigger male, and she would have a limited protective tendency toward her independent male offspring and would raise male off springs to be dependent like her. Nature had provided for this type of balance. We reversed nature by burning and pulling a civilized nigger apart and bullwhipping the other to the point of death, all in her presence. By her being left alone, unprotected, with the **MALE IMAGE DESTROYED**, the ordeal caused her to move from her psychologically dependent state to a frozen, independent state. In this frozen, psychological state of independence, she will raise her **MALE** and female offspring in reversed roles. For **FEAR** of the young male's life, she will psychologically train him to be **MENTALLY WEAK** and **DEPENDENT**, but **PHYSICALLY STRONG**. Because she has become psychologically independent, she will train her **FEMALE** off springs to be psychologically independent. What have you got? You've got the nigger **WOMAN OUT FRONT AND THE** nigger **MAN BEHIND AND SCARED**. This is a perfect situation of sound sleep and economics. Before the breaking process, we had to be alertly on guard at all times. Now, we can sleep soundly, for out of frozen fear his woman stands guard for us. He cannot get past her early slave-molding process. He is a good tool, now ready to be tied to the horse at a tender age. By the time a nigger boy reaches the age of sixteen, he is soundly broken in and ready for a long life of sound and efficient work and the reproduction of a unit of good labor force. Continually through the breaking of uncivilized savage niggers, by throwing the nigger female savage into a frozen psychological state of independence, by killing the protective male image, and by creating a submissive dependent mind of the nigger male slave, we have created an orbiting cycle that turns on its own axis forever, unless a phenomenon occurs and re-shifts the position of the male and female slaves. We show what we mean by example. Take the case of the two economic slave units and examine them close.

Frozen Psychological State of Independence

Let's break this down.

Trauma is the result of exposure to a stressful event or events that causes one's sense of security to be destroyed or lost, leaving a person feeling helpless and vulnerable to this traumatic event, which would continue to happen at any unexpected time. Any situation that causes one to feel alone and overwhelmed can be classified as traumatic. The harm or torment does not have to happen to the observer physically, however the harm becomes psychological to the observer. The more helpless, frightened, powerless, or paralyzed one feels, the more one is traumatized. It has been noted that there is a biological response to trauma: the picture captivates the eyes, the heart skips a beat, the breaths hold on for dear life, the body turns numb, and the person finds herself activating at the highest alert as she becomes witness to something so terrible and hard to imagine.

Psychological State

We know that the word *psychological* comes from the word *psychology*. Psychology relates to: the science that deals with the mental processes and behavior; emotional and behavioral characteristics of an individual, group, or activity; subtle tactical action or argument used to manipulate or influence another; and the branch of metaphysics that studies the soul, the mind, and the relationship of life and mind to the function of the body. I think the third meaning serves much explanation to how the masters manipulated the minds of the slaves to accomplish their purpose. This manipulation was a mental condition in which the qualities of the state of mind of the slaves was a constant one; even though this state was a dynamic one, one would never know this by the actions of the slaves. This creates a somewhat manic state, which is abnormal. It relates to a bipolar state. This psychological chain has been passed down from generation to generation as a curse and has created a coping mechanism in our black females today, which has been very much misunderstood.

Frozen Psychological State

Let us examine this frozen psychological state of independence a little closer; this will assist us in having a better understanding of what the female slave was experiencing, and what the masters were trying to accomplish. As outlined, the master's objective was keeping the body but taking the mind. This sixth principle is all about destroying the black man before the black woman. He was her protection. Once this was done through the various processes outlined here, the black woman was now frozen in a psychological state of independence.

Anytime the word *frozen* is used, it is referring to a thing being stopped solid. With the female slave, she was traumatized by what she saw. This brought about a fear that was so great she consciously submitted herself to the master so she would not have to remember what she had seen and felt. The freeze response is an automatic, reflexive reaction that occurs when an individual is faced with a threat that is perceived as overwhelming. It is the last resort the individual turns to in order to survive. This reaction can in some instances serve as a constructive means of survival. As humans, our survival instinct is strong and driven. It is not controlled by our neocortex, which focuses on intent or reasoning. This often results in feelings of helplessness, which is often experienced by individuals after one is faced with trauma. One is unable to tell oneself to not freeze. This is controlled by instincts and may serve as an optimal response at the time.

Recent theories suggest that the act of freezing is a consequence of the nervous system's reaction to a traumatic experience. This freezing response is also said to result in an individual freezing for a period of time without being aware of it. When fight or flight is not an option, an individual may freeze. The autonomic nervous system goes into a freeze response, and the body is unable to move.

The body may also react in a manner that allows the person to play dead, so as to protect the person from further harm from threat. These are all survival instincts, which are performed in reaction to the stress or danger and which may be performed without the person's conscious awareness. However, in the case where the person freezes or reacts passively, the likelihood of experiencing post-traumatic stress disorder symptoms in the future is increased.

With this detailed information (thanks to the Cape Peninsula University of Technology), let us now relate it to the female slave. Let us take a look with her and see what she sees. The female slaves see the strong men being torn apart by horses, having their arms and legs ripped away from their bodies. She sees them tar, feathered, and set on fire. She sees them lynched by the neck from trees, and even then, sometimes their bodies are set on fire. She sees them beaten with whips until they wish they were dead. She sees the dogs turned on them, and much more. All of the acts are in your history books. Personally, I feel traumatized. How do you think you could have handled this traumatic chain of events? Think about it for a moment. They were in a place that they were not familiar with; they had nowhere to run, nowhere to hide. The color of their skin would prevent them from being able to hide, and of course there was the language barrier. The female slave had no choice but to submit to the master. Her love for her male seed and her husband caused her to submit to the master—and teach the other men to also submit. Absorb all this for a moment. It took strength to endure this process. The female slaves endured for the sake of the lives of their male slaves. Even though they endured much, they were still bound by the bonds of family. Despite it all, our ancestors survived!

Independence

How does the need for the female slaves to feel independent fit into the completion of this reversal process for the slave owners? The masters understood how important the female slave factor was for good economics. He understood that by destroying her dependence on the strong slave male, she would move from to this frozen psychological state of independence. In addition, she would train her female offspring to be psychological independent. This sense of independence was simply a mental state; they really were not independent. Yet their need to believe and feel they were independent and controlling things was a part of the plan. Their goal was to please the masters, have their daughters be independent, and have their males become independent. This worked. Therefore the female slaves became the gatekeeper for the masters.

This has perpetuated itself in our black culture today. This gatekeeper business has been seen on many jobs today: usually a black female running to the boss behind everyone's back and telling on other black employees.

I guess they could be referred to as the Female Uncle Tom of today. Don't forget it was a black woman who stabbed Martin Luther King. She probably got her instructions from her employer. According to the press, she claimed she had been looking for him for five years. Yeah, right! She probably got her instructions from a modern-day slave master. Not only did this process make the female slaves feel independent and the males feel dependent, but it also caused a division between the men and women.

The three stages of development in our lives are as follows.

(1)   Dependence: one relied on aid and support, and requires assistance from others.

(2)   Independence: one does not depend on or is controlled by others; it is associated with oneness.

(3)   Interdependence: the dynamic of being mutually and physically responsible to others, sharing a common set of principles; it implies unity.

It is very obvious that some black women are still stuck in the state of independence, and we need to understand why. There is a psychological war going on inside of you when it comes to submitting to a black man. The reason is centered on a couple of things. First, his ability to protect you was destroyed, and you do not hold the respect for him that you should. Second, because of the curse that went along with this frozen psychological state of "independence," you are afraid of becoming dependent, losing yourself, and putting your guard down to trust to a black man. It is like there is a war going inside our minds, and sometimes it overrules our hearts. We want black men in our lives, yet we need to make some changes too. Understand that this too was by design. This curse has to be broken. When we as a people can truly understand that we were not programmed to be together in a loving environment, we can start to work on the problems of separation and division that we face today.

We can understand that we have lived under a matriarch system; this is the system that was our heritage from Africa. It is a system of family, group, or state governed by a matriarch, a system of social organization in which descent and inheritance are traced through the female line. Yet we live in a patriarchal society controlled by men with a disproportionately large share of power. Can you better see the conflict between independent black females and dependent black males? Matriarchies and patriarchies do not work together and will never work positively, because both neglect and suppress the true benefits and natural abilities of the opposite gender. It is time for us as a people to see our past, our present, and our future. We need to see and examine ourselves, the way we live, the way we love, and the way we die. We need to find out why we react, think, and believe in the things we do. We need to examine ourselves and find out whether the chains and the whips that enslaved and controlled our ancestors have the same effect on us. Today we have psychological chains that have orbited from our ancestors. The question is, do we have the courage to break off the chains of our oppression and embrace real freedom? It is then and only then that we as black men and women can come together with the love and appreciation that once existed for each other, walking in a state unity.

Mission Accomplished

Naturally, the female slave did not want to see the male slaves tortured, beaten, and killed. Neither did she want to think about her young sons suffering the same. part of the masters' plan was to reverse the rolls of the female slave with that of the male slaves. That is exactly what they set out to accomplish. They used the same concept on the slaves that they used to tame a wild horse. The female horse will eat out of the master's hand when broken in, and she will teach her young colt to eat out of the master's hand. The same mission was accomplished with the black woman. In an effort to protect her males offspring, she would teach them to be good workers, physically strong yet mentally subdued. Then she taught her daughters to be like her, independent. At least, that was what she thought. Because she was frozen in a psychological state of independence, she would raise her male and female offspring in reversed rolls.

Let's spell it out. There is so much misunderstanding today about the strength and control of the black woman. Let's clarify where it started. "For the fear of the young male's life, she will psychologically train him to be mentally weak and dependent but physically strong!" "Because she has become psychologically independent, she will train her female offspring to be psychologically independent." "You've got the niggar woman out front and the niggar man behind and scared, this is the perfect situation of sound sleep and economics."

> Once this has been accomplished, the slave owners can sleep soundly because out of frozen fear the woman stands guard for the slave owner. Okay, let's do a simple review-by having the niggar female savage into a frozen psychological state of independence, by killing the protective male image and by creating submissive dependent mind out of the niggar male, they have created an orbiting cycle that turns on its own axis forever, unless a phenomenon occurs and re-shift the position of the male and female slaves.

By now you should be saying, "Wow! Now I have some understanding why there has been so much contention between black men and black women." Let the light bulb come on fully, because there is so much more to this that relates to where we are today. In my opinion, these two sections of the letter have an even greater impact on our lives today. Look around you. You have been seeing it and didn't know from where it originated. In fact, what you have been seeing or looking at has been orbiting since slavery. What am I talking about? Do you have any idea? Have you been following me with this letter? This whole idea is so wide and so deep. I will start off by talking about myself.

I am now inserting the rest of the Lynch Letter because I believe the last two sections covered the main objections of the slave owners and had the most devastating effect on the slaves. I believe that the sections to follow are simply showing us the implementation of the process, definition, and understanding, and further how they reinforced and carried out the perpetuating cycle.

The Negro Marriage

We breed two nigger males with two nigger females. Then, we take the nigger male away from them and keep them moving and working. Say one nigger female bears a nigger female and the other bears a nigger male; both nigger females—being without influence of the nigger male image, frozen with a independent psychology—will raise their offspring into reverse positions. The one with the female offspring will teach her to be like herself, independent and negotiable (we negotiate with her, through her, by her, negotiates her at will). The one with the nigger male offspring, she being frozen subconscious fear for his life, will raise him to be mentally dependent and weak, but physically strong; in other words, body over mind. Now, in a few years when these two off springs become fertile for early reproduction, we will mate and breed them and continue the cycle. That is good, sound and long range comprehensive planning.

A Little History on Slave Marriages:

Most slaves' owners encouraged their slaves to marry. It was believed that married men were less likely to be rebellious or to run away if they were married. Some masters favored marriage for religious reasons and it was in the interest of the plantation owners for women to have children. Child bearing started around the age of thirteen, and by twenty the women slaves would be expected to have four or five children. To encourage child bearing some plantation owners provided women slaves their freedom after they had produced fifteen children.

It has been recorded that several slaves did not want to marry girls that belonged to their same plantation. Reason, they could not bear to see her ill-treated. Neither did the slave males want to live in the same house with the wife, for he had to endure the continual misery of seeing her flogged and abused without daring to say a word in her defense.

Slave marriages had neither legal standing nor protection from the abuses and restrictions imposed on them by slave owners. Slave husbands and wives without legal recourse, could be separated or sold at their master's will. Couples who resided at different locations were allowed to visit only with the consent of their owners. Slaves often married without the benefits of clergy.

Basically the marriage ceremony in most cases consisted of the slaves simply getting the master's permission and moving into a cabin together.

There were some ceremonies that the masters participated in and were done by the clergy. In most cases these slaves worked in the house and were given special treatment. On the other hand some slaves had their own ceremony of "jumping the broom" which in their eyes consummated their marriage.

Note; the children of any marriage where the husband was on another plantation, belonged to the plantation owner of the female slave. Sometimes the masters would purchase the spouse of the slave to keep them together. All of these adjustments and interactions were allowed because it made good economic reasoning. Once again; the female slaves will raise their female daughters to be like her independent and raise her male sons to be dependent like their fathers and male slaves. Thus these practices continued the cycle of both the males and females being subdued for the masters. Now the masters have created an orbiting cycle that turns on its own axle forever, unless a phenomenon occurs and re-shifts the position of the male and female slaves.

I recommend reading parts 6 and 7 for even an more detailed description of what the master's plans and concepts were based upon, as well as their plans of implementing these concepts into the lives of God-created humans. Part 7 of letter speaks for itself and sums up the intent of the whole Lynch letter of creating a slave.

<u>Warning: Possible Interloping Negatives</u>

Earlier, we talked about the non-economic good of the horse and the nigger in their wild or natural state; we talked out the principle of breaking and tying them together for orderly production. Furthermore, we talked about paying particular attention to the female savage and her offspring for orderly future planning, then more recently we stated that, by reversing the positions of the male and female savages, we created an orbiting cycle that turns on its own axis forever unless a phenomenon occurred and re-shifts positions of the male and female savages. Our experts warned us about the possibility of this phenomenon occurring, for they say that the mind has a strong drive to correct and re-correct itself over a period of time if it can touch some substantial original historical base; and they advised us that the best way to deal with the phenomenon is to shave off the brute's mental history and create a multiplicity of phenomena of illusions, so that each illusion will twirl in its own orbit, something similar to floating balls in a vacuum. This creation of multiplicity of phenomena of illusions entails the principle of crossbreeding the nigger and the horse as we stated above, the purpose of which is to create a diversified division of labor; thereby creating different levels of labor and different values of illusion at each connecting level of labor. The results of which is the severance of the points of original beginnings for each sphere illusion. Since we feel that the subject matter may get more complicated as we proceed in laying down our economic plan concerning the purpose, reason and effect of crossbreeding horses and niggers, we shall lay down the following definition terms for future generations. Orbiting cycle means a thing turning in a given path. Axis means upon which or around which a body turns. Phenomenon means something beyond ordinary conception and inspires awe and wonder. Multiplicity means a great number. Means a globe. Crossbreeding a horse means taking a horse and breeding it with an ass and you get a dumb, backward, ass long-headed mule that is not reproductive nor productive by itself. Crossbreeding niggers mean taking so many drops of good white blood and putting them into as many nigger women as possible, varying the drops by the various tones that you want, and then letting them breed with each other until another circle of color appears as you desire. What this means is this: Put the niggers and the horse in a breeding pot, mix some asses and some good white blood and what do you get? You got a multiplicity of colors of ass backward, unusual niggers, running, tied to backward ass long-headed mules, the one productive of itself, the other sterile. (The one constant, the other dying, we keep the nigger constant for we may replace the mules for another tool) both mule and nigger tied to each other, neither knowing where the other came from and neither productive for itself, nor without each other.

Controlled Language

Crossbreeding completed, for further severance from their original beginning, **WE MUST COMPLETELY ANNIHILATE THE MOTHER TONGUE** of both the new nigger and the new mule, and institutes a new language that involves the new life's work of both. You know language is a peculiar institution. It leads to the heart of a people. The more a foreigner knows about the language of another country the more he is able to move through all levels of that society. Therefore, if the foreigner is an enemy of the country, to the extent that he knows the body of the language, to that extent is the country vulnerable to attack or invasion of a foreign culture. For example, if you take a slave, if you teach him all about your language, he will know all your secrets, and he is then no more a slave, for you can't fool him any longer, and **BEING A FOOL IS ONE OF THE BASIC INGREDIENTS OF ANY INCIDENTS TO THE MAINTENANCE OF THE SLAVERY SYSTEM.** For example,

if you told a slave that he must perform in getting out "our crops" and he knows the language well, he would know that "our crops" didn't mean "our crops" and the slavery system would break down, for he would relate on the basis of what "our crops" really meant. So you have to be careful in setting up the new language; for the slaves would soon be in your house, talking to you as "man to man" and that is death to our economic system. In addition, the definitions of words or terms are only a minute part of the process. Values are created and transported by communication through the body of the language. A total society has many interconnected value systems. All the values in the society have bridges of language to connect them for orderly working in the society. But for these language bridges, these many value systems would sharply clash and cause internal strife or civil war, the degree of the conflict being determined by the magnitude of the issues or relative opposing strength in whatever form. For example, if you put a slave in a hog pen and train him to live there and incorporate in him to value it as a way of life completely, the biggest problem you would have out of him is that he would worry you about provisions to keep the hog pen clean, or the same hog pen and make a slip and incorporate something in his language whereby he comes to value a house more than he does his hog pen, you got a problem. He will soon be in your house.

Well, we know that this section of "Controlled Language" was well put together, and that the statements that were stated above are true. However, this is where they truly failed. The slaves learned the language, learned how to communicate, and learned how to read, count, and write. Then they ended up in the house. In many cases, they ended up running the houses. From taking care of the children to cleaning the house, cooking the meals and serving them, going to the store, and shopping for things needed at the house. Some of the black women were given full charge of the house. The slave owner was soon able to see that these slaves were peace-loving people, and if they were treated right, they would be devoted. "Being a fool is one of the basic ingredients of any incidents to the maintenance of the slavery system." Through their own communication, some began to figure out the plot to keep them enslaved. Thanks to the female slave who was smart enough to outsmart the slave masters and put their full trust and faith in this system to work unconditionally. As previously stated, nature has a way of correcting itself, and no matter how the slave owner tried to treat the slaves as less than human—or as indigenous, as they put it—the slaves overcame every obstacle presented before them and of course made their way to physical freedom. The question that we will deal with later is, "Do we have psychological freedom?"

Now that you have reread this letter and regained your lost composure, you may say, "Wow!" Yes it is a lot to take in and digest at one time. I believe that reading this letter once is not enough to truly get a good understanding that will stick in your memory. I suggest you digest the content of this letter in sections or in parts. The content of this letter is deep and full of substance. My God, it was carried out, and it still works in some form in our lives today.

In the following pages, you will find that I have incorporated parts 2–7 of the Lynch letter to discuss what I believe to be the key ingredient of the process of making a slave—that is, the black woman. I truly believe that this process of making a slave could not have been possible without the characteristics and traits that already existed in the black woman. I see no need to repeat the content of parts 2–7 as I continue to write about the key factors then, which are still the key factors today. The white slave masters saw these qualities then, and they know that they still exist today. Keeping division between black males and females was their objective then, and it is still their objective today.

It has been said that "when you teach a woman you are teaching a people; because whatever she knows she passes it to her children." This was why the woman was so important to the white slave masters. The slave masters understood this concept. They made reference to the female horse and colt. The masters knew that they had to pay close attention to her and her offspring. They knew the necessity to break her so that she could not look to the strong "niggar man" for strength and support. Then of course they would break the strong nigger man by cruel treatment. They knew they had to destroy his pride and self-esteem, and render him helpless. The "niggar woman" could no longer look to him for support and strength. Thus this concept was implemented.

The masters knew that the original order (God's order) of the family is the man, the woman, and then the child. They knew by causing these roles to be reversed, it would cause things to be out of the natural order, and they would be able to control the salves. They knew by design that this reversal implemented would cause the black woman to be raised to be mentally strong. She would have to be strong to mentally endure all the torturing, abuse, hurt, and pain she saw with her own eyes. It was a necessity to be strong to protect her male seed and men; there was no other choice, other than destruction. Some took that route. They would rather die than endure the pain and suffering for them and their loved ones.

By implementing this process, the masters put the slaves in a position where they had to totally depend on them for everything. The slaves no longer had a home, a culture, a family, or a language, and they lost much more. All they had was the slave masters. The white master's message to the black woman was, "trust me, teach your children to trust me and your men, and I will allow you 'independence' in the midst of your bondage." It was this implementation that caused the black woman to feel independent yet psychologically in a frozen state of dependence. That dependency has been for the black woman to depend upon the white man, not the black man. This trait of dependency of black women on white males is still orbiting today in black America.

Now, don't get me wrong, I truly understand that the white man has provided you with jobs and all the things that you have needed to exist today. There are simply not enough black enterprises or businesses that can offer enough jobs to make a dent in the unemployment of black America. However, we are living in a time where we must create positions or employment for ourselves. God created us in His image, and He is a creator. Therefore we are creators too. It is time for black Americans to reinvent themselves. We are talented and creative; we can do it. Seek God, and the god within you, and receive a revelation of your talents and abilities. Do I need to remind you about the known black inventors? Or what the blacks have already contributed to society? This information is available for you. "Seek and you will find, knock and the door shall be opened unto you." Let us eliminate all excuses.

CHAPTER 9

The Black Female

Role Reversals: Once again, I am going to refer to a popular movie to reflect how this role reversal has carried over into our lives and way of living today.

Baby Boy

This movie was written and directed by John Singleton. If you have not seen this movie, I suggest you purchase it. However, if you are black you could probably ask any young black person to borrow a copy. These movies are collected, along with Singleton's other movies. Therefore I am simply going to give you a quick overview of the movie as it relates to my point of role reversals.

The plot of the movie is about a twenty-year-old black male named Jody who lives with his mother, Juanita, in South Central Los Angeles. He is unemployed and spends most of his time with his unemployed best friend, Sweetpea. He does not appear to be interested in becoming a responsible adult. Obviously, Jody has never left home, even though he has romantic relationships and two children. He has a son with his girlfriend (Yvette) of seven years, and he has a daughter with a girl (Peanut) with whom he cheated on his girlfriend and who lives with her mother.

The movie starts off with Jody's girlfriend Yvette having an abortion. Jody is trying to be sensitive to his girlfriend; he refers to himself as daddy to the girlfriend. He proclaims that he just wants to take care of her. Then he asks to use her car; remember that his mode of transportation is a bicycle. Yvette has a job, a car, and an apartment.

Jody is driving down the street and sees younger guys riding their bicycles down the street. He refers to them as his "little homies." Of course, there is association because he truly hasn't grown up yet himself. He really sees himself like them, in addition to the fact that he is somewhat of a bicycle mechanic. His bicycle is the best in the hood.

Then Jody drives Yvette's car to his baby mama, Peanut. He catches her in the shower and tells her to come fix him some food. In the next scene, Jody is eating, and Peanut is rolling a joint. Her mother pulls into the driveway with his baby in the back seat. He goes out to meet the grandmother and get the baby. He gets the baby out the car and proclaims, "I knows how to take care of a baby … as well as making pretty babies." It is obvious that the grandmother of the baby is not pleased with Jody or her daughter's actions, however she loves the grandbaby.

After this scene, a sequence of events take place between Jody, the girlfriends, the friend, the car, and his mom asking Jody how Yvette was doing and expressing her dissatisfaction by giving him the money for Yvette to have the abortion.

In another scene, Jody comes home and finds a truck in the driveway with all types of gardening tools on it. He goes to the back yard and finds his mother, who could be his sister because she looked so young, planting a garden. She explains her intent to him about the garden. Then this big hunk of a gardener comes out the house. She introduces him to Jody as her friend Melvin, and they let Jody see that they have sexual attraction to each other. The mom lets Jody know that she plans to keep him around. "Mama has to have a life too." Jody tells his friend about the mother's boyfriend, and he is now concerned that they will want him to move out because of their need for privacy.

Trademark Made In America

From this point on, another sequence of events take place. Yvette's ex-boyfriend, Rodney, is released from San Quentin State Prison and returns to the neighborhood, to move in with Yvette—yet he does not like Jody or Jody's son, JoJo. A number of negative things happen that are centered on this scenario, from rape to murder. Then there are the issues are at Jody's house with Melvin. From this point forward, Jody had to wake up and man up. He has a lot to learn, and it is happening quickly—and the hard way. It takes another strong black man who is persistent to cause this change to take place.

At the end of the movie, Jody has now become a mature man, realizing that his mom's relationship with Melvin is a stable one, and that Jody has a family of his own that he needs to protect and take care of. If you have not seen the movie, I recommend you view it. Most young black people have seen it. Yet younger people have no clue of the deeper meaning of this movie; they simply identified with the characters in the movie.

Now, let us examine the overall message, how I perceive the reversal of roles, and how they played out in this movie. But first, let us take a look at the subliminal message that was sent.

This movie starts off showing a fully grown black male still in the womb of the mother, with the navel cord still connected. There is a lady by the name of Dr. Frances Cress Welsing; she has a theory about the black man in America. She says because of the system of racism, the black man is this country has been made to think of himself as a baby and as a not yet fully formed being who has not realized his full potential. To support her claims, she offered the following. First of all, what does a black man call his girlfriend? Mama. What does a black man calls his friends? His boys or his niggas. Finally what does a black man call his place of residence? The crib. I am in agreement with this statement, however I would like to add that this movie is a perfect example of role reversal as outlined in the Lynch letter.

Jody's mom supported her son's immature way of thinking, up to the point of her getting a man of her own. In other words, there was something that the mom was getting out of her mother-son relationship with the absence of a man of her own. This is a prime example of the mother subduing the son as weak minded, accepting it and supporting it until it no longer served her purpose. Then she wanted him to grow up, be a man, and stop acting like a kid. To Jody, loyalty was to his mom instead of his baby's moms. The baby mamas needed Jody to be a man and leave his mom so he would be devoted to them.

We still find this scenario happening today. One baby mama had a job, car, and apartment, and she needed her man (Jody) to be strong. She knew that she had need for a strong man, and her emotions were so connected to Jody that she hated him because of his weakness. Now, we know the word *hate* is connected to the person who is loved. We feel hate when we want something from the ones we love, and they refuse to give it to us; that emotion we feel is expressed as hatred. However, after a sequence of events centered on Jody, he was forced to grow up and be a man.

I have spoken to several black women today, and they have expressed that there are a lot of black men who are still at home with their mothers. The females have a job, a car, and a house or apartment, yet the black men are still making excuses on why they are still at home with their mamas. Once again, the black woman has moved out in independence, and the back male is still dependent. Their attitude is, "Why should I leave home, where I have a roof over my head and food to eat, only to go into an unknown situation that may not work out? I know my mother loves me. I don't know about you." What they are really saying is, "My mom has put up with my laziness and my excuses all these years, and this may not fly with you."

The flip side? The boy's mother is single and has become complacent with having her son in her life. Her son has become her man. The mom tries to sabotage every relationship the son gets into, and no woman is good enough for her son. Another woman will take her son away from her. Once again, the son is not always saved by a man coming into the life of the mom. Sometimes it takes the mother to see that she is losing her son (as the man in her life) before she will even open up any avenues to allow in another man. We see these examples time and again not only with the mother and the son, but also with the father and the daughter.

Another movie is *Act Like a Woman, Think Like a Man*. The mama's boy is referenced in this movie, and once again there's the protection the mother had over the son until she allowed someone into her life—again, a displaced relationship.

Another movie is *Jumping the Broom*. The mother is giving her life to the well-being of her son; even when he has moved on, she is stuck and does not see that she is stuck. She still sees him as a young boy who needs her. She does not want to lose that relationship. Instead of looking at it as not losing a son but gaining a daughter, all she can see is losing her son to another woman, and that woman replacing her. Again, we are talking about the displaced relationship between mothers and their sons. There are those mothers who never had a personal relationship with a man because of this displaced relationship. They replaced the displaced relationship they had with their sons, and they are now lonely and sickly. Some have died of loneliness. Some have died of cancer or a broken heart. I know that there are families where you can identify with the mother and son relationships.

Also we as black people know that mothers, grandmothers, and girlfriends will do whatever is necessary to protect the black male. In most cases it is a single-parent resident. The father (strong male role) is absent, and therefore the object of attention to the female is her sons. It is important to understand where this originated from: "The Making of a Slave." Now, I ask you this question: Do you know any scenarios where the roles were reversed, and we are now talking about mother and daughters?" The answer is no. That old saying, "behind every successful man is a good woman (mothers included), and behind every successful woman is herself," still rings true today.

The black mother didn't have to worry about her daughters because the black woman's independence (psychologically) was demonstrated. The black female has moved out and gotten jobs, apartments, cars, education, and promising careers. The white man has provided the door of opportunity for the black female in many ways. However, along with this state of independence comes the thought of "Unless I can find a black man of my equal status, I don't need a man." Meanwhile, the white man is in her ear, saying, "What can the black man do for you?" Again, this is to keep division between the black male and female.

Did you think it strange that the mama's boy in the movie *Act Like a Woman, Think Like a Man* fell in love with the woman with the child? I have a theory about that too. A mother knows how to nurture because she nurtures her children. The mother is usually not selfish, because a mother knows how to give and share. These virtues are good and can easily be spotted and identified by a male who has had a close relationship with their mother. They desire to continue a nurturing relationship, which they have grown so close to. They desire to spend their time with someone who is into them and knows how to precipitate the warmth of love in return. These men have found that a single woman over the age of thirty-five is usually pretty set in her ways and self-centered. This is not a bad thing, however the need should simply be understood.

A New Role Reversal

We are already aware that there is a large number of single households in black society. There are a number of single fathers who take care of their children where there is the absence of a mother, or there is joint custody between the father and the mother. This is a somewhat usual situation for the mother, yet the fathers appear to take on the real mother role and bring about another division between the black man and black woman by not allowing another woman in his life. There are so many conditions to a relationship that are centered on the child, and it almost makes it impossible to have the right kind of male-female relationship. He knows that he wants a woman in his life, however he has moved from the father role to the mother and friend role with the child. Therefore, he is now putting the child before a natural relationship with a woman. He puts his relationship with a female somewhat on hold, and he puts his relationship with the child first.

Now, don't get me wrong—he is supposed to love his child, to provide for protect that child. Yet this relationship is now out of character for the child and the parent. The relationship is out of order. The father treats the child like they are friends, and he allows the child to make decisions in their relationship. He can't understand why he can't keep a relationship with another woman. The child wants the father to get back together with the mother. The mother has moved on with her life, yet the father is stuck somewhere between being a man and a father. This too is a role reversal. The father has taken on the character of the mother instead of finding a woman who will love him and his child. He is stuck. He tries to date, and because the mother of the child already knows how sensitive he has become with the child, she causes disruptions with the father and any potential relationships. The father allows it for fear of having problems with the baby's mother. This causes a woman in a potential relationship with him to see him as weak. She'll ask, "Would this continue if we were married?"

I have heard of dates being broken because the baby's mother wanted to go out, and she didn't have a babysitter, so she manipulated the baby daddy. He broke his date with the potential female. I hope the men who read this can see something is wrong. Once again, the black woman needs a strong man. She needs a man who can be a father and still be a man. She needs a man who knows how to keep the child in the child's role through love. She needs a man who will not allow the baby's mother to dangle the child like a carrot in his face in order to use him and take advantage of his love for the child. She needs a man who can love her and have a relationship with her as well as the child. The order of the family is the man, the woman, and the child. Remember that during the making of a slave, the order was altered to the woman, the female child, then the man or male seed.

What is it about this new issue of men waiting for their kids (usually girls) to turn eighteen and go off to college before the men get into a relationship? There used to be an issue of women bringing men into their homes where there were children, and for fear of abuse or molestation, the women would wait until the children were graduated from high school or left home before a man was brought into the house. Black men, there is something that you need to see here. Does this fit your description, or the description of someone you know? Women, are you still being the controlling bitch that some Black men say that you are? If so, get out the way. Allow your baby daddy to be a good father and a happy man, and then he can be a better father. You didn't want him for whatever reason, so stop interfering with him finding a new relationship.

There is much more that can be said on this subject, however the object of this book is to bring to your awareness where we are today as it relates to where we came from, and why.

By Design

By Design: Today, many black men do not have any male influences in their lives to show them how to be men and take care of a family. In black America, over half of all households are run by the mothers alone. Again, this was by design. I remember years ago, when a black single mom could not get assistance from the county or social services if the father was in the picture. She had to tell the social workers that she didn't know where the father of the children was, so she could get benefits to live. The husband or father of the children would live there and hide if the social worker came to the house. Heaven forbid if the social worker came unannounced and caught the male there, because the mother would be cut off from her benefits. This was to keep the black male feeling helpless and inferior.

By Design: The black neighborhoods had liquor stores spring up in every heavily populated area. The liquor stores were originally owned by whites and Jews; and then later Asians and other nationalities. Once again, every nationality but blacks had the opportunity to make money off the black neighborhoods. The underprivileged, downtrodden black males would be the main customers who would patronize the liquor stores.

By Design: The next big event to keep the black man enslaved was selling drugs to the black communities. This was introduced to blacks by whites, because who knows the black communities better than the blacks? Here, we are going down another path of destruction and enslavement with drugs. The drug dealers appeared to be living high in wealth. They made it seem like this was a good thing to do: have money and don't be broke—sell drugs to your own people.

By Design: We now no longer have communities with just alcohol and drugs; we have another ingredient added. We now have communities and families that contain drug addicts. The alcoholics get drunk to forget their problems, and then they usually sleep it off. They are unable to hold down jobs, are usually homeless, and usually beg for money to buy food and more alcohol. Now we have been introduced to a new menace to society: the drug addict. These addicts steal and sometimes kill to support their habits. Thus crime is on the rise, raging in inner-city areas.

By Design: Black people are robbing and killing black people. Today, millions of black men across the United States are incarcerated for drug- related crimes. Some have jail time that exceed the time required for the crime. Today, prisons for black males and females are simply a modernized slavery system, and the prison represents the new plantation. Incarcerate as many black men as possible; this will once again leave the black women without black male support.

By Design: Black men who are gay or bisexual have turned into a growing trend. There is an origin to every action. There have always been gay men and women among all cultures. However, there have always been a higher number of whites in the gay community than blacks. Now, we find the number of blacks has increased dramatically. What caused this increase? Black people by nature have been God conscious. Today, that concept appears to have been overridden by more value being put on doing what feels good. If it feels good, it must be right. This concept of doing what feels good is following in the footsteps of the less than God conscious people. Or perhaps it's the fact that we desire to be so much like the white men and women that we refuse to allow our God consciousness to be our guide. However, we as a people need to have an education and stability in order to be awakened to who we are.

By Design: There is the prison system, where you can go in like a man, become interrupted, and become gay. Or because of shame, you come out and try to be the man you once were, but now you are in the closet and bisexual. They are living this secret life that can never remain a secret. This is from where the spread of HIV to the black female has come. This is the reason for the high percentage of HIV among black males and females today. There is so much more I could say on this subject, however this subject is not the focus of this book. However, I will say spiritual deception comes to us in many ways. It is called deception because we are deceived and are unaware. Again, it's by design to keep division and separation between the black male and female.

By Design: The white man has exploited the athletic black males in football, basketball, baseball, and track and field. In addition to sports, we have the entertainment field: actors, singers, and whatever performances that make people wealthy. I am referring to the black and white counterparts. When the blacks become wealthy, so do the whites who exploit them. Now that the black male has become wealthy, he is made to feel that he has arrived at the white man's level. By design, the black man who has reached the white man's status now takes on the ultimate female, "the beautiful white woman." This idea has been planted in the minds of so many black men since slavery.

However, now that money has caused them to reach this status, the white men are willing to share their white women; after all, what they are really saying to you is, "You deserve the best of the best, because white is better than black. We, the white men, will look over your black skin and only see the money that you are making for us." The white woman means to the black man, "I have totally arrived. I can now have the once forbidden fruit."

By Design: So many of our black men have taken for their spouses non-black women. Once again, this practice is leaving the black female without that strong black man to look up to. The white man is still subduing the black man by keeping division between the black man and the black woman. The saying "United we stand; divided we fall" has been the plot of the white man with the black men and women from the beginning of slavery, and it is still being carried out today.

The white man understands the value of the black woman. He understood her strengths as well as her weaknesses. It was the white masters who had the black women in their homes cooking, cleaning, and breastfeeding their children. On occasion, the black woman was used to satisfy the lustful needs of the masters. Of course, one cannot keep having sexual relations with another and not start having some kind of compassion and feelings. Don't forget the black women had babies for the masters too. The white man's objective was to never let the white woman know his true attraction to the beauty of the black female. We know love has no color. We know from history that there were times and places where the white man fell in love with the black woman, and of course it had to be hidden for her safety, or even his. The white man could be labeled a nigger lover. Nevertheless, the white man's need to control caused him to not only subdue the slaves but also subdue the white woman.

Madame C. J. Walker was the first female millionaire. She happened to be black. She was a millionaire before any white females were millionaires. She was a millionaire before women were given the right to vote. How did this happen? Did white women have any ideas that could have led them to become millionaires, or were they simply eye candy on the white man's arm? It really does not matter, because the most important thing was that the white man didn't try to stop C. J. Walker from fulfilling her dreams. They did not see her ambition to be a threat to them. Therefore, C. J. Walker was a self-made millionaire. I must share these words with you that she wrote, because they should encourage you.

"I am a woman who came from the cotton fields of the South. From there I was promoted to the washtub. From there I was promoted to the cook kitchen. And from there I promoted myself into the business of manufacturing hair goods and preparations ... I have built my own factory on my own ground." She would often say; "I got a start by giving myself a start."

She started selling door to door in 1900 and was incorporated in 1911. Women were not given the right to vote until twenty years later, August 26, 1920.

Oprah, whom we all know and love, is a black female. She has been the wealthiest female in America for many years. Once again, she could not have risen to the top and gotten to this place in her life with just her talents and abilities. She had to have been backed or supported by a wealthy white man (or Jewish man) in some form.

There are many prosperous black men and women in America today. I would venture to say that 90–95 percent of them have been financially backed by non-blacks. That's just a guesstimate. I am aware that there are many black- owned and black-operated businesses in America today; I praise and thank God for them, and I hope there would be more to come. We are a creative people and are living in a time where we need to depend on ourselves and pull from that creativity that is from God.

By Design: We are a race of people already so full of insecurity. How can we see the truth and be set free of the lies and deception that we have faced all of our lives? These lies and deception have propelled itself from generation to generation for hundreds of years. This is the question. Then can the reality of truth be accepted once it has been founded and established.

CHAPTER 10

Conclusion: The Curse Must Be Broken

Earlier in chapter three, you were given information facts regarding a curse. It was my intention to prove to you how a "curse" went out with the William Lynch letter. This curse has propelled the decree that went out over three hundred years ago and caused a slave mentality to be created and continue for generations, unless something remarkable happens to change its course. I am certainly not the first person to identify these issues, and I know I will not be the last. There are many people to reach. But we must not take this issue so lightly. We have the power to break the perpetuating cycle of our generation and future generations.

There are those of you who feel this curse does not apply to you. You may feel this way because you are a Christian and believe that you are covered with the blood of Jesus. Let me clarify that there are many scriptures in the Old Testament relating to curses. In the New Testament, we are told that Jesus Christ not only came and died on the cross for our sins, but He also conquered Satan so that we can be set free from curses. This is true, however Jesus gave His servants the power to break curses in His name (Gal. 3:13). This means that we must do something about it, and we have been given the power to do so. Let me say to you, and to the church world, that so much of the Church's teaching is, "If you are a spirit-filled child of God, you are not subject to demonic curses, possession or attacks. I have news for you." It is time to wake up.

The New Kings James Bible says in Hosea 4:6 that my people perish because of a lack of knowledge. Ignorance is not bliss. How can you fight a battle that you don't know exists, because you can't see it? How can you defeat an enemy that is attacking you when you do not believe that this enemy has power or control over you? In 2 Corinthians 2:11, it states "lest Satan should take advantage of us; for we are not ignorant of his devices." The scriptures clearly state that God's people will suffer many things and ultimately end up in captivity if they continue to walk in sin and ignorance. This certainly includes curses. When this has been brought to their attention, Christians will often comment, "God would not hold me responsible for something that I am not aware of. God would not allow a curse to come on my life when I was not aware that I was doing something wrong." Well, guess what? God holds us all accountable for everything that is in His Word, and this information is in His Word. I believe the main reason most Christians are not ready to deal with this issue is because once they accept it, they are accountable to do something about it.

James says in Revelations 2:7 and Matthew 11:15, "he that has an ear to hear, let him hear." This phrase appears seven times in the gospels, or eight if you count Mark 4:23. Christian church members often never seek to find out anything on their own and are totally reliant upon the teachings that come from the pulpit. Some members never exceed beyond the teachings of their leader. This is okay and acceptable if their leader continues to grow and be enlightened, and passes that knowledge down to the congregation.

Understand that it is not my intention to bash pastors, however the Church is still known as the sleeping giant. Some pastors' top objective is to keep their members in fear and subjective to them, and therefore they teach according to niceness. They do not want to make any waves with the members and keep them feeling good about themselves and the church they attend. That's their security blanket.

This walk is an individual one. It is time to wake up and become educated on how the adversary works. Yes, there is an adversary. Whatever your belief is, whether it is negative energy created by you or the source of all creation, negativity will work against you without a doubt. Do you truly understand what is going on in the invisible? I will go into this subject more in another book. For now, our concentration is on breaking this curse.

I spent a lot of time covering the issue of hair. I recently saw a posting of a black woman who had purchased hair from India and had it sewn into hers. Shortly afterward, she started to see changes taking place in her life. Her marriage broke up, her finances when downhill, and she appeared to be somewhat out of character. She had taken the hair out, but she had paid so much for it that she was still holding on to it. All roads led to the hair having a curse on it, which was passed on to her. The curse was broken, the hair was destroyed, and ultimately her life returned to normal.

What is my point? We know some of the third-world countries worship idols, and a lot of them have a dislike for Americans. I have also personally witnessed items being purchased in Africa (and brought back to the United States) that had curses placed upon them. These curses can cause a decline in health, finances, relationships, and other catastrophes. Once identified, the curses have to be broken. This is real, people.

God gave us the authority—let us use it! Command the curse of fear, distrust, envy, servitude, poverty, insecurity, low self-esteem, psychological independence, control, loneliness, physical abuse, stealing, murder, unfaithfulness, adultery, inferiority, role reversal, and rejection. Reject the Willie Lynch curse, the slave trade curse, and curses from Africa. As you read this book and other thoughts come to you, add them to your list. Command them all to leave you because they are not from God and have no place in your life.

For all you black men and women who are afraid of dogs (no matter how small), swimming (afraid of drowning; never learned how to swim), and horses (afraid to go near one, let alone ride one), this fear comes from the curse of slavery. Another fear is represented by the distrust of all black people and only trusting white people. These fears are brought on from your ancestors' fears, and they should be broken off your life and your seed.

Once again, there is much to be said about curses. After you have broken the curses of your life, command the enemy to return what was taken from you! Command it to be return and restore it times a thousandfold.

It is time to seek a solution to your own oppressive conditions. It is time to disassemble the negative propagandas perpetrated by our slave masters during our ancestors' enslavement. But we cannot seek our solutions from Europeans—that is, white America. We must seek it upon our own Afrocentrism. We already have the power within us. It is there without the name of Jesus, the Church, or the Bible. You have been made to feel that without those three, your life is like filthy rags, and you are hopeless. Not true! The power is within you; it's in your ancestors. Simply speak the word with confidence and faith, and watch it work for you.

Eurocentrism versus Afrocentrism

In order for African Americans to overcome the psychological shackles of racism, one must understand the philosophy of Eurocentrism versus Afrocentrism. The transatlantic slave trade indoctrinated Africans and African slaves with Eurocentrism. This philosophy is centered on the idea that civilization began in Europe and that Europeans are superior to other races, especially Africans. Can you imagine that we were made to believe that civilization started in Europe? We know better. Afrocentrism challenges Eurocentrism and says that civilization started in Africa. Therefore, Afrocentrism was designed to reconnect African Americans with Africa. I am by no means advocating that we, a black America, return to Africa. Everybody came from somewhere. Simply understand that you had a place of origin, and it was Africa.

Now, let us pray for our motherland and our sisters and brothers there, because they are still enduring a lifestyle that is subpar to what a human should be subjected to. Here in America, we must understand that racism is real, and we must understand our needs consciously and unconsciously in order to be accepted by European Americans and white America. We must know who we are, hold our heads up, and walk proudly in who we are.

Roll with It!

Why trademark? Let us define the word: "a symbol or other identifying mark that identifies a product as having been made and/or sold by a particular business."

I like this definition because it identifies us as black people. We were made here in America by the white man. We are the closest race of people that there is to the white people. Here in America, we have patterned ourselves after them; they became our role models. They gave us their last names. We are the black version of them. We are the perfect imitation of a white man and woman. Out of all the nationalities of people in this world, we are the only culture that has taken on the names of our slave masters. Think about this. All other cultures have their own native surnames. Wow! Have you ever met or heard of a Chinese person whose last name was Jones or MacGreggor? No! Yet we as black American do not have our African surnames. Why? We do not know our surnames because they were taken from us, along with our vibrant African history.

Now that you know the truth, are you going to search your ancestry's history back to Africa and find out your real name? Probably not. You will simply continue to roll with the one you have. But at the least, you should think about it.

I asked a friend, "Did you know Jesus was black?" Then I waited for her response.

It was, "It doesn't matter what color he was, as long as he saved us from our sins."

My response was, "But it does matter! It matters because you have accepted the lie that the white man has given to the world. The blue eyes, blond hair, frail Jesus is not the description of our Lord and Savior Jesus Christ. That's all you know, and that's good enough for you, so you are willing to roll with it. Why would you want to believe the lie, with the truth not mattering to you?"

It is true that the color of His skin has nothing to do with your sins being saved. But what is the real question here? Why did the white man have such a need to cover the truth? It was in order to take away your heritage, so that you will never know who you really are or who your ancestors are. Therefore you can remain in a state of helplessness. Now, how would you feel if I told you that all the characters in the Old Testament (and many in the New Testament) were of black lineage, and that other nationalities came later? How would you feel? Does this tidbit of information make any piercing to that trademark that is carved in stone in your mind about yourself and black people? Are you going to keep on rolling with the lie? Are you going to stay in your safety net of dependency on the white man? Or are you going to stick your chest out and say; "I need to know more!"

I recently attended a gospel concert. The word *gospel* lets you know it was put on by black people with black Christian artists. It was great—so anointed, and so inspiring. The first thing I noticed was out of approximately one hundred people performing on stage in the choir, every female had on a wig or a weave. There was one hairpiece, and one lady with braids. They were all beautiful. They sang great, however none of these women chose to wear their own hair, with the exception of the two women previously mentioned. Once again, I thought about how the hair industry is a sixty-billion-dollar industry propelled by black women. How are we paying the owners of these shops so much money? We are paying for their homes and cars, and sending their kids to college. Yet we can't afford a house or a car, and college is far out the picture for most of us and for our children. Let me say that I have already observed 98 percent of the women who entered the auditorium were wearing wigs or weaves. *Trademarked*, I thought to myself as I observed them. Then to my surprise, at intermission time, one of their sponsors was a weave import company with an advertisement for hair. To top that off, they gave a number to text from your cell phone to win tickets to another concert, or two packs of Brazilian top-quality hair. I heard a sound of excitement from the auditorium. In the dark, I could see cell phones light up as women texted the number to have an opportunity to win the Brazilian hair.

Black women and young ladies, are you going to keep on rolling with this hair that only belongs to you because you purchased it? Are you going to keep contributing to this sixty-billion-dollar giant that you have created, or are you willing to give the hair that God has given you a chance? Are you willing to take back your identity? Are you willing to crash this industry that you have created through your demand? Are you willing to starve it out? Remember, God created you—your lips, your hair, and your skin. God does not make mistakes. Once again, I am reminded of the story of Adam and Eve in the Garden of Eden, after they had eaten the fruit. They were hiding from God. Then God spoke, and said Adam, "Where are you?" (Gen. 3:9). Adam confers he was trying to hide from God; he was afraid because he was naked. God said "Who told you, that you were naked?" (Gen. 3:11). Adam blamed Eve, and Even blamed the serpent.

Now, God is asking you this same question: who told you that you were not beautiful? Who told you the color of your skin, the texture of your hair, your wide nose, and your thick lips were not beautiful? God did not tell you this! He said, "You are made in My image. You are My sheep, and you have gone astray. It is time to return to Me. You were robbed of your birthright; now it is time to take it back. If the Israelites were enslaved for over two hundred years in Egypt and still remained Israelites, and if other European cultures from the twentieth century survived from ancient Greece and Rome, how much less could be expected from My black children in America, who were enslaved only for a couple of centuries? Don't forget your heritage. If I told you in My Word that My hair was as lamb's wool and My feet were as brazen brass, are you ashamed of me?"

Black America, I am simply trying to educate you and encourage you to allow the light bulb to come on in your mind and heart. "Truth brings about freedom." Black people, you are physically free and mentally in bondage.

John 8:32 says, "And you shall know the truth and the truth shall make you free." This statement is truly stated, however the knowledge of truth alone cannot set one free. Freedom comes when the truth is received, accepted, and acted upon. It is only through the application of truth that you earn freedom and change; otherwise, if you have never acted upon the knowledge, you are stuck in the same place you were before you came into the knowledge. So I ask you again: Are you ready to be set free, or will you keep on rolling the same way you have been going your whole life? Can you still deny the truth?

Once again, I would like to add that working with our own hair can be time-consuming. I started wearing my natural hair shortly after I started writing this book. I used to wear weaves for the convenience. I went to visit a family member at a secured facility. I had just had the fresh beehive braided and had on a quick weave that I had made; it was a whole head weave. The sergeant at the desk asked me if it was sown in. I could not lie, so either I could not go on my visit, or I had to do one of two things: have the beehive unbraided, or have the weave sown in. Probably having some stitches shown around the cap of the weave would have been the quickest. I was so annoyed that I had to do this that I took the braids down. My hair looked like Angela Davis's Afro. I put on makeup and eye shadow and then strutted back up to the desk. The head officer said to me, "That's what I am talking about, that looks great." He added, "I don't understand why you black women don't wear your own hair." Of course, he was white. I simply smiled.

But since then, I have been working it. I get a lot of compliments, even when I don't think it looks that great. Ninety percent of the compliments I get are from other nationalities. What you black women don't get is that others think we are beautiful without the hair hanging down our backs and looking like the Europeans they have seen all their lives.

Yesterday, I walked into the library; I had a french roll up the back and a bun that came to my face like the old-style hairdos of the twenties. I also had on my makeup. This handsome white man said, "How are you?" I said I was fine. He said, "I know you are fine. I just wanted to know how you were feeling." I blushed and thought, *How cute.*

Another day, I had simply brushed my twisties back into a french roll, pinned them up with hairpins, and went into a computer repair shop. The young, handsome man touched my hair and told me how pretty it was. Again, he was not black. So my question to you is: Do you not get it? They know the truth that we don't even know about ourselves. We are desired too. Understand that I am not opposed to a backup plan for a bad hair day, but I have chosen to roll with the natural—no more perms for me. My hair is growing and healthy. I believe the key to looking cute for women is wearing makeup and trimming their eyebrows. Of course, we all know that beauty generates from the inside and radiates outward. Make sure your heart is right.

I know it is a lot to absorb at one time. Take your time and absorb it slowly. A big boulder in time will crack if you keep chipping away at it. Changes will take place in your life if you keep chipping away at it. The first thing is to see and recognize the need for change and simply move forward to do it, "make the effort!"

Relationships

Black women and black men should stop bad-mouthing and putting each other down. You have been told the truth about the created division that has propelled itself from slavery time until now. It is past time to walk in that truth. Learn to be a better communicator. Talk to each other, even if it makes you vulnerable. Remember that life or death is in the power of the tongue. Send out positive seeds regarding each other so that those positive seeds will come back to you. This law of the universe really works. What can we really expect from our children when confusion is going on beneath the surface? They see it and don't really understand it, yet they act upon something to offset the turmoil and confusion that is going on inside of them.

The question is, are you going to do something positive about making changes, or are you going to continue to keep rolling with the way you have been rolling all these years? Remember, insanity is when someone continues to repeat the same cycle and expect a different outcome. Now, please understand that I am not opposed to interracial marriages and relationships. However, there is certainly unresolved issues between the black female and the black male that should be addressed.

I would like to conclude by referring to a recent popular movie among our people, with the message that was being conveyed in this movie. Remember, as I previously stated, I am aware that the movie writers are sending an underlying message to the viewers.

Django Unchained

Written and directed by Quentin Tarantino, this movie won two Oscars, with another twenty-eight wins and fifty-three nominations in other film industry award shows. This movie is a western that took place in the backdrop of post–Civil War. It is an action-packed movie, and it appears that each actor was specially designed for the character. They portrayed their parts to the fullest. This movie was brutal, bloody, terrifying, hilarious, and inspiring.

My synopsis of this move is as follows. The movie is about a slave who had a brutal history with his previous slave owner. He was sold separated from the wife he loves, and he ended up working with a German bounty hunter (Schultz), who was somewhat unorthodox about slavery. Schultz was on the trail to find and capture the murderous Brittle Brothers. Schultz was told that Django was once on that plantation and could identify them. Therefore, a relationship developed between the two of them. Schultz offered Django his freedom if he would help him catch the brothers, dead or alive—preferably dead. Django agreed and told Schultz about his wife, including how much he loved her and wanted to find her. They made an agreement that if Django stayed with Schultz through the winter, Schultz would give him one-third of all money collected from their bounty hunting and would help him find his wife.

The Brittle Brothers were killed, and Schultz and Django made it through the winter. The movie moves forward with a number of scenes associated with the mentality of the slaves and their masters, the lifestyles during slavery on these plantations, the brutality and torture of the male slaves, the whipping and beatings of some of the female slaves, the Mandingo fighting, and an example of a real Uncle Tom. The analogy told about the brain of a slave for servitude, and the movie showed the luxury of some of the slave women who were used for pleasure. The scenes in this movie are very factual.

How timely it was to see this movie, which was produced in 2012, three hundred years after the William Lynch curse. This movie gives the audience a visual of today's view on some of the lifestyles during slavery and the mentality of the slave owners. In an interview, Tarantino refers to his thoughts of slavery here in America as the sins of Americans that have truly not been accounted for.

Django, unchained and free, did not allow anything to stand in his way of getting the woman he loved. He was a strong man, a former slave. He was determined to get to the wife whom he loved at any cost. He accomplished his goal and in the end destroyed the plantation, which represented the foundation of slavery. At the end of the movie, Django and the woman he loved rode off into the sunset to freedom.

This movie was not like *Roots*. *Roots* left black viewers feeling disappointed when the movie ended. When Chicken George had the opportunity to kill the master that had caused so much havoc and didn't do it, and he said, "If I killed him then I would be as bad as he is," this left whites feeling good and blacks "once again feeling angry and not feeling vindicated for what our ancestors had been through." *Django Unchained* sent out a message of vindication that gave the black viewer a good feeling at the end of the movie, a feeling of, "It's about time." It puts fear in the hearts of some white viewers because it did not leave them feeling good.

To the men and women of black America, I believe that this movie is sending a message to us. We are free. We have been unchained for hundreds of years. Free yourself from the mental bondage; break the curse off your life. Black men, your black women need you; they need you to be a strong man. Remember that the image of you was destroyed years ago. Black women understand the role reversal and the psychological state of independence that has been implemented with you, and it has gone from generation to generation through you and your offspring. With this understanding of truth, you will have a better understanding of why you do and think the way you do about many things in your life, including but not limited to your daughters, your sons, black males, black women, the workplace, and the black community as a whole.

It is time to recognize, understand, and acknowledge the bondage of slavery that has been hovering over our lives. It's time to destroy the oppression of the curse of slavery. It is time for true freedom!

IN LOVING MEMORY OF

My sister, Rev. Cherrye Ann Ross Cunnigan,
who was with me in the incubation stages of this book.
We spent many hours together at her home, the doctor's office,
and the hospitals. My sister had cancer and had to take regular chemo
treatment, with various tests taken. We had many hours of conversation about
many subjects, however I worked on the research for this book when
we were separated. She was always encouraging me to not allow
anything to stand in my way of finishing this book. I promised
her that I would complete it and get it published.
She felt that it was a much-needed subject
to address at such a time as this.
I will keep her in my memories
for the love and support
she gave to me.
Thank you!

I have kept that promise!

ACKNOWLEDGEMENT

This page is dedicated to the people that I would like to humbly thank!

To Diane Wayne, MS, RDN - My dear and very close friend. Thank you for the encouragement and spiritual support you provided me from the beginning to the end, it was much needed and appreciated. Thanks you!

Friends and Associates:

To the barbers at the barber shops I frequented; you know who you are. Thank you for allowing me the opportunity to share the content of this manuscript with you and your clients. The feedback as well as your input was enjoyed and appreciated. We know that the local barber shop is a place that will keep the education and knowledge flowing to our people and the communities. Finally, the book is here. Keep the content alive. Thank you!

To the beauticians at the beauty salons I frequented; you know who you are. Thank you for allowing me the opportunity to share the contents of my manuscript with you. I know and understand how and why the relationship between the African American man and the African American female was the focus of interest and discussion. Since the dynamics in the beauty salon is somewhat different from a barber shop; I encourage you ladies to stay in touch with the truth and pass the knowledge on to all that are willing to listen regardless of age, culture and gender. You have the ability to teach those that you encountered; to exchange truth, knowledge and understanding as to how and why we as African American's here in these United States got to where we are today. The beauty salon can be that place. Thank you!

To all the people I have encountered over the last 2 years that I have shared this manuscript with; you know who you are. I want to thank you for your feedback and your desire to see all cultures educated to why we as African Americans do the things we do. Thank you for desiring to see this book become a part of the education system. Understand that sometimes, there is a need to create one's own education system. The book is finally here, keep the information flowing. Thank You!

ABOUT THE AUTHOR

Where she grew up:

She grew up in a small southern town in Chattanooga, Tennessee, in a quiet community call Shepherd.

Family History:

She was the youngest of five siblings, one sister and three brothers. She grew up in a loving home with both parents.

Children:

She has given birth to six children that are alive and well. In addition, a host of children that has grown up and still calls her mom.

Education:

She has earned a BS Degree, Doctorate of Divinity, and Masters of Biblical Counseling. In addition, several certificates: Reiki, Time Line Coach & Trauma Release Specialist, Neuro-Linquistic Programming, Life Coach, Communications & Life Mastery Specialist, Clinical Hypnotherapist, and Hypnosis Mastery.

Accomplishments:

She has performed the ceremony for multiple weddings and special funeral services. She has a heart for helping people and has prayed for many people that have been healed of various conditions. In addition, she is an entrepreneur. She has owned several businesses and multiple pieces of property. She has successfully provided a home and training for teen girls through the foster system and has been recognized by the school district as an outstanding parent.

Struggles / Overcome:

Her greatest challenge has been to re-invent herself after the real estate market collapsed. She had been out of private enterprise for 10 years prior to running a real estate and mortgage company. What do you do when you are over qualified and nobody wants to hire you? This caused her to pursue her heart's desire which was writing and continuing to assist people in their spiritual growth and to become whole. She has stepped up to the plate to move forward. Her philosophy for life has been, "giving up" is NOT an option. Where there is a will, there is a way.

Beliefs about God:

She believes that there is a God and she has faith in that belief. She also believes that the bible can serve as a book of discipline and that all cultures have one. However, she believes that God is in you therefore the knowledge that one needs to be guided by can be pulled from within. "Greater is He that is within, than he that's in the world." She is a firm believer in Universal Laws, which were the original laws. That is what she desires to teach.

What gives her strength and encouragement?

She believes that she can accomplish whatever she set out to do. She believes that patience, endurance and faith will bring whatever she send out to come back to her. She believes in the laws of seed, time and harvest and that keeps her encouraged.

Mary Ross Morris

Other writing project coming in the future:

There will be many more writings to come. She has knowledge in a variety of areas and is looking forward to writing about many subjects that she believes would be a blessing to many people.

Contact information like website or other projects you do like promoting book, consulting, etc. will be provided.

TRADEMARK MADE IN AMERICA: "BLESSED" NOT CURSED!
Written by Mary Ross Morris

Many African descendants in America bear the cruel legacy of enslavement. During the years of the slave trade, African men and women were captured and brought herein chains, tortured or killed for the smallest infraction, with no knowledge of the language, no personal possessions, and few familial connections. But Morris believes that added to these factors was an insidious plan to make slaves even weaker and unlikely to rebel. It was detailed in what is known as the Willie Lynch letter. This document was first brought to light in the 1970s and said to be a transcript of a speech given by Lynch, a plantation owner from the British West Indies, to a group of white slave owners in Virginia in 1712. In it, Lynch, whose name became synonymous with the term for murdering blacks, describes the method for managing and controlling African slaves. Mere violent punishment is ineffective in the long run, he stated. What was needed was a psychological restructuring of the slave's deepest values.

In order to control slaves, according to Lynch, white owners would punish black men severely in the presence of their wives and womenfolk. This would cause mothers to raise their sons to be obedient to the master, docile, but physically strong so that they could do their work as expected. The female slaves were rewarded with attention as they developed these traits, so they would become naturally hard-working, even ambitious, to please the master and raise their daughters to do likewise. The master would also use such issues as skin color to keep the slaves in a state of mistrust and competition among themselves, rewarding lighter-skinned folk and shaming those with a darker complexion. The traits described give a surprisingly accurate view of some of the problems that African Americans still experience. Morris wishes her fellow African Americans to acknowledge these weaknesses inculcated by arrogant, selfish white slave owners. Through understanding these psychologically implanted barriers, modern African slave descendants can eliminate them now and forever.

Morris, an educator, therapist, and inspirational speaker, makes her argument cogently, examining the racial stereotypes that are accepted within American black society through such elements as well-known films, court cases, and even mainstream Christianity, which has always painted Jesus as a white man when he was arguably of a darker complexion. She urges black women to celebrate their beauty, especially their hair, which has been denigrated by comparison with white characteristics. She encourages African American men to develop more favorable relationships with darker-skinned women instead of looking at light complexion as a prize to be won as proof of manhood. She casts a strong light on biblical history, making clear her belief that early Israelites would have been dark-skinned Africans and that African civilization existed long before white Europeans. She relates many of the current ills of American black society to the model of the Lynch letter—which can be considered a curse upon black Americans—and hopes that thoughtful readers will begin to erase that negative influence and start proactively to seek the blessings of true freedom and equality.

Reviewed by:
Barbara Bamberger Scott
The US Review of Books

Printed in the USA
CPSIA information can be obtained
at www.ICGtesting.com
LVHW040746230324
775320LV00002B/305